THE TAME MILLS OF
STAFFORDSHIRE

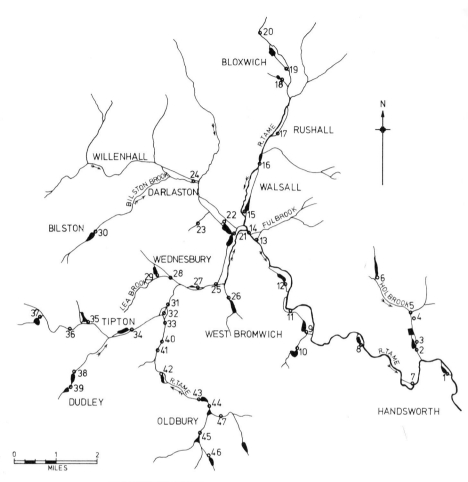

STAFFORDSHIRE TAME WATER MILL SITES

KEY

Plan 1: 1. Holford Mill. 2. Holbrook Paper Mill. 3. Holbrook (Gough's) Corn Mill. 4. Holbrook (Birch's) Wire Mill. 5. Holbrook (Birch's) Rolling Mill. 6. Barr Mill. 7. Perry Barr Mill. 8. Hamstead Mill. 9. West Bromwich Old Forge. 10. Sandwell Mill. 11. Jone (Joan) Mill. 12. Bustleholme Mill. 13. Friar Park (Bescot) Forge. 14. Walsall (Bescot) Bloom-Smithy. 15. Walsall New Mills. 16. Walsall Town (Malt) Mill. 17. Rushall Mill and Furnace. 18. Cole (Coe) Pool Mill. 19. Goscote Mill. 20. Clock Mill, Pelsall. 21. Wednesbury Forge. 22. Peck Mill. 23. Sparrow's Forge. 24. Bentley Mill. 25. Wednesbury (Wystie) Mill. 26. Hateley (West Bromwich Hall) Mill. 27. Wednesbury Bridge Mill. 28. Lea Brook Mill. 29. Willingsworth Mill. 30. Bilston Mill. 31. Gold's Hill Mill. 32. Tipton Forge: Moore's Mill. 33. Eagle Foundry. 34. Tipton Bloom-Smithy. 36. Coseley Blade Mill. 37. Parkes' (Persehouse's) Hall Mill. 38. Castle Mill. 39. Priory Mill. 40. Fisher's Mill. 41. Sheepwash (Greet) Mill. 42. Dunkirk Mill. 43. The Mill (Abney's). 44. Bromford Mill. 45. Oldbury Green (Hill's) Mill. 46. Langley Mill. 47. Oldbury (Blakeley) Mill: Shenston's Mill.

The
Tame Mills
of
Staffordshire

by

D. DILWORTH
M.A., B.Sc., F.R.G.S.

PHILLIMORE

1976

Published by
PHILLIMORE & CO., LTD.,
London and Chichester
Head Office: Shopwyke Hall, Chichester,
Sussex, England

ISBN 0 85033 216 8

Text set in 11/12pt. Baskerville
PRINTED AND BOUND BY
W. & J. MACKAY LTD.

CONTENTS

LIST OF PLATES

(between pages 54 and 55)

LIST OF FIGURES

LIST OF MAPS AND PLANS

ACKNOWLEDGMENTS

No work of this type can be carried out without the writer making use of the interests, enthusiasms, researches and knowledge of many who have trodden at least part of the path before him. Such store of facts as may be found here has been amassed only by the co-operation of many friends and acquaintances.

It is to Mr. E. Lissimore, historian of West Bromwich, that I owe my introduction to the story of the early days of the Black Country, and to a number of friends and colleagues of the Birmingham Branch of the Geographical Association that I owe a more specific interest in the local industries and water power.

I am indebted to Lord Bradford for permission to inspect and quote from documents in his possession at Weston Park.

For information, suggestions and assistance in many ways, and in varying degrees, my thanks are due to Mr. Stitt, County Archivist of Staffordshire, Messrs. M. Greenslade and G. Baugh, editor and assistant editor of the *Victoria County History of Staffordshire,* Mr. F. A. Barnett, historian of Sedgley, Mr. J. F. Ede, historian of Wednesbury, the Librarians, and their staffs, of Birmingham Assay Office, Birmingham Reference Library, Dudley Central Library, Kidderminster Central Library, Walsall Reference Library, Warley Central Library, Wednesbury Central Library, West Bromwich Reference Library, William Salt Library, Hereford County Record Office, Stafford County Record Office, Dr. C. Sands, Mr. and Mrs. D. Ching, for their work on the maps, and the many who supplied something from their fund of local knowledge.

I have attempted to supply the facts so far as they are available and to avoid surmise, intelligent or otherwise. For avoidable omissions and errors of interpretation I accept entire responsibility.

D. DILWORTH

January 1976

Hence dusky iron sleeps in dark abodes
And ferny foliage nestles in the nodes,
Till, with wide lungs, the panting bellows blow,
And, wak'd by fire, the glitt'ring torrent flows;
Quick whirls the wheel, the pond'rous hammer falls,
Loud anvils ring amid the trembling walls;
Strokes follow strokes, the sparkling ingot shines,
Flows the red slag, the length'ning bar refines;
Cold waves, immersed, the glowing mass congeal
And turn to adamant the hissing steel.

Dr. E. Darwin, Economy of Vegetation

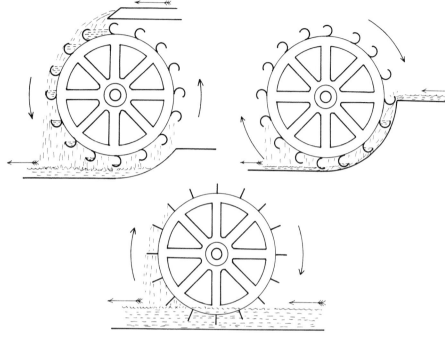

Fig. 1: Types of Water Mill. 1. Overshot Wheel. 2. Breast Wheel. 3.
3. Undershot Wheel.

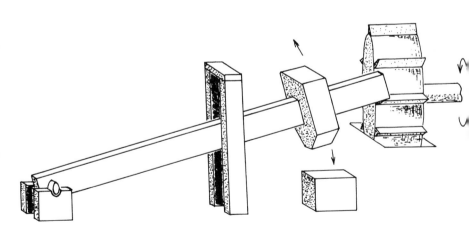

Fig. 2: The Forge Trip-hammer.

PART ONE

PREAMBLE

There was the Black Country unrolled before you like a
smouldering carpet. You looked into an immense hollow
of smoke and blurred buildings and factory chimneys.
There seemed to be no end to it. In the vague middle,
dominating everything, was an enormous round white
tower, which I afterwards learned was a new gasometer.
It looked larger than anything else in sight . . . There was
the scream of a locomotive; there was the clanking of
bumped wagons; there was the long pu-u-ushing of a
train gathering speed . . . I descended into the vast
smoky hollow and watched it turn itself into so many
workshops, grimy rows of houses, pubs and picture
theatres, yards filled with rusted metal and great patches
of waste ground, which was as shocking as raw sores and
open wounds . . . Industry has ravished it; drunken storm
troops have passed this way; there are signs of atrocities
everywhere; the earth has been left gaping and bleeding;
and what were once bright fields have been rummaged
and raped into these dreadful patches of waste ground . . .
We had climbed to the top of a hill and a cold wind was
blowing over it, bringing dust and grit and filthy bits of
paper. On one side was a stretch of high brick wall,
which some posters told me was a sports ground. On the
other side were some patches of waste ground and
some decayed allotments where the last green rags of
gardening were showing. Further along was a yard filled
with rusted parts of motors and scrap iron . . . My friend's
warehouse was in—shall we say—'Rusty Lane', West
Bromwich. He keeps sheets of steel there, and no doubt

any place is good enough to keep sheets of steel in; but I do not think I could let even a sheet of steel stay long in Rusty Lane. I have never seen such a picture of grimy desolation as that street offered me. If you put it, brick for brick, into a novel, people would not accept it, would condemn you as a caricaturist and talk of Dickens. The whole neighbourhood is mean and squalid, but this particular street seemed the worst of all.

Such was the Black Country seen through the eyes of J. B. Priestley in 1933.

*   *   *   *   *   *

Today, 40 years on, should one come to sit beside the Castle Keep in Dudley, a slightly different view would be presented. The smouldering carpet has been almost extinguished. The changing industrial pattern, and enacted 'smokeless zones', have reduced the density of the heavy grey canopy which for so long hid much of the squalor beneath from the distant viewer. The depletion and final extinction of economic local resources of coal, iron ore and limestone have enforced industrial change. One solitary blast furnace still stands sentinal at Bilston. Gone is much of the heavy iron and steel work of former days. A rash of white asbestos roofs over the landscape marks the spread of new factories catering for lighter industries. No longer the once white gasometer dominates the scene, but is rivalled by the dozens of lofty concrete boxes, providing a battery-hen existence for their occupants, or out-topped by the vapour-plumed cooling towers which announce the location of the power stations at Bloxwich and Ocker Hill. The closer view reveals that much has gone yet much remains. The clamorous steam engine has been replaced by the almost silent electric or diesel locomotive on the few rails that have been preserved. Red-brown tracks or long ribbons of weed mark those abandoned. The canals, once the arteries of the Midlands, are now the oily black ditches being filled with old prams, bicycles and motor tyres. A new age has brought the motorway, stretched across the country on its

concrete legs like some gigantic fossilised prehistoric
centipede. Most of the spoil heaps of colliery and
furnace have been removed to fill the waterlogged marl
holes and so provide yet more space for house and factory.
Yet this has not eliminated the waste areas of 40 years
ago, but merely changed their sites: for the vast yellow
crawling machinery of today demolishes whole streets
overnight, to provide yet more space for redevelopment,
but in doing so leaves wide areas of brick and rubble in an
already unlovely environment. While many areas of small,
crowded, blackened, paint-starved, decaying property still
exist, it seems that every available space is grabbed for
housing, mainly local-authority owned, and while prefer-
able to that it has replaced, is still monotonous in its
repetition. Some things do not improve. The cold wind
still brings its bits of filthy paper, but the present
generation finds more paper, and plastic, with which to
litter its streets. In a more affluent age aerosol paint
containers have replaced chalk as the armament of the
graffiti writers, and aged cars and bedding are considered
fitting adornment for any open space or quiet lane. The
inhabitants seem determined to resist the insidious advance
of civilisation.

The aspect of the Black Country is changing; but then
it always has been. It was changing when Priestley drew
his gloomy picture less than half a century ago. No
longer was it the throbbing vigorous metallic heart of
England that it had been in the middle of the last
century. Most of the collieries were already abandoned;
most of the numerous blast furnaces were closed. Gone
were the Wilkinsons and Bagnalls, the Parkes and Hick-
mans. Foundry work and engineering were in a depressed
state. The running iron no longer painted red the night
sky. Most of the many brick-kilns were cold and the
marl holes filling with stagnant water.

If we could put back the clock some 500 years
and from beside the Keep look over the same Upper
Tame valley, we should see a scene different in detail
but yet recognisable in outline: before us the rounded

top of Barr Beacon, far to the left the forest-clad Cannock
Chase. Closer at hand the churches of Walsall, Wednesbury,
West Bromwich and St. Peter's, Wolverhampton, each on
its hill top, might be seen rising above the foliage of the
still heavily-wooded basin. Surrounding each church and
covering the slope of the hill, a village of thatched-
roofed, mud-walled cottages. A little aloof perhaps the
more substantial moated, half-timbered manor house.
Other hamlets, such as Bilston, Bradley, Willenhall and
Darlaston, lacking churches, clung to the slopes of minor
eminences avoiding the flood-prone banks of the Tame.
Below the hamlets, pushing back the forest walls, were
the common fields, the Church Fields, Priest Field,
King's Hill Field and Monway Field, each worked in
strips by the peasant following his wooden plough and
ox team. From the woods arose the spiral of smoke
telling of the charcoal burner pursuing his labours. The
sounds were those of rural England; the murmur of
pigeons; the harsh call of homing rooks; the occasional
ringing of the church bell or the call to prayer from the
Priory of Dudley or Sandwell; the cry of children. To
these must be added the ringing anvil of the village smith,
the steady rumble from the mill beside the stream, the
tinkle of harness bells from the train of pack-horses
along the woodland track and, most significant, the sound
of pick and spade, for coal and iron ore were already
being won from shallow holes in the ground near to
Wednesbury, Bradley and Sedgley.

So different the scene to the casual glance, yet there
were the seeds from which grew the Black Country of
more recent years. The iron and coal were already
being worked though it was not for another 200 years
that coal was to be used for the manufacture of iron.
Without the use of coal, large-scale iron work was
impossible. The charcoal iron industry devoured the
forests and provided the raw material for the small
forges and the hundreds, if not thousands, of nailers'
shops that were to crowd the living space of the slowly
growing villages and hamlets.

The increase in size and number of the forges, the advent of the furnace in the late 16th century and even more, the coke-consuming furnace of a century later, all demanded more power than the muscle of man or beast could provide and until the arrival of steam power, it was to the water mill, inefficient as may be, that man turned. The growth of industry was steady but it was only comparatively recently that it succeeded in obliterating the remains of the rural scene. Many open fields and commons were enclosed, usually piecemeal, during the 18th century, around Bilston, Darlaston, Bentley and Walsall. Wednesbury was not completely enclosed by 1800. Aldridge was enclosed by 1795, West Bromwich in 1801, Perry Barr in 1811 and Walsall Wood as recently as 1866. As late as 1796, William Pitt was extolling the virtues of the soil for growing of cereal crops and noting the timber growth at such places as Sandwell, Perry Barr and Bentley, admittedly on private estates.[1] At the same time he decried the use of water mills as a causing of flooding and hence the disuse of good agricultural land and urged that all mills should be removed to towns and coal and steam power be used both for corn-milling and iron manufacture.[2] He could not have imagined that in a few years such power would be used, but that the towns would have spread and swallowed what he wished to preserve.

Even about 1820 the Rev. Townsend wrote of Wigmore (in West Bromwich) as 'The wild retreat, Where winds the pathway with the winding stream'.[3]

> And o'er the swelling waters brown,
>   That eddy as they flow,
> Elm, Oak and Ash, their mighty arms
>   Fantastically throw.

* * * * *

> Yon rude stone steps, the cottage girl
>   Descends to fill her pail.

Poetic licence? Maybe, but the Tame was not yet the black, sewage-laden stream that it became later, polluting the neighbourhood with its stench. It still provided the power for a number of water mills; the mills which over the centuries had fostered the growth of the iron industry, the basis of the Black Country we know today.

So little trace of these mills, or the part that they played, remain today, that it is urgent that the little should be recorded before it is lost for all time.

NOTES

1. William Pitt, *Agriculture of Staffordshire* (1796), p. 59.
2. *Ibid.*, p. 124.
3. Rev. Townsend, *Wigmore*. This poem is contained in Jos. Reeves, *A History of West Bromwich* (1836), p. 52.

PART TWO

WHAT THEY WERE

A water-mill, for the purpose of this work may be defined as a building housing machinery for which the motive power is provided by a wheel which is turned by the agency of water. The term mill is used loosely and is not confined to the grinding of corn.

In this country it was common practice for the wheel to rotate in a vertical plane, driving a horizontal shaft; a contrast to many in eastern Europe where the wheel is horizontal as in the case of the celebrated '14 mills of Jajce' in Bosnia. The wheels themselves are driven in several ways. The most efficient is that which uses the potential energy of the water, the latter being led by trough or duct and allowed to fall on to the wheel at a little beyond top dead centre. The water, caught in cups or 'ladles' on the perimeter of the wheel, causes that side to sink under gravity, the water being emptied out as the ladle approaches the lowest point of rotation. Such wheels rotate with the top of the wheel moving in the direction of the flow. This type is known as an 'overshot' wheel. Such a wheel will continue to operate as long as a flow is maintained. The second type is the 'undershot' wheel. In this case the ladles are usually replaced by boards or 'paddles' fixed to the circumference, parallel with the driving shaft. The lowest part of the wheel is immersed in the stream or a channel and the wheel is driven by the kinetic energy available. This method is less efficient and is variable being dependent on the velocity of the current and hence on the weather and the state of the stream. Since the overshot wheel

necessitates the availability of water at or above the level
of the top of the wheel, it is obvious that it can only be
used in an area of marked relief, usually in a steep valley,
while it is equally obvious that the undershot type would
also be most effective where a steep gradient is available.
The problem is to find the most efficient arrangement in
an area of gentle gradients. The usual solution is a
compromise, the 'breast-wheel'. In this case, the head
of water being insufficient to permit of the impact being
at the top of the wheel, the water is delivered as high as
possible on to the side of the wheel, which is equipped
with ladles as in the overshot variety. The direction of
rotation is such that the bottom of the wheel moves with
the current. If the head available is insufficient for the
impact to be above the halfway position we have the
'low-breast' type. Here it is usual for the wheel to rotate
in a reasonably close-fitting pit so constructed that the
floor of the pit is curved up, to follow the curvature of
the wheel, on the headrace side of the wheel. In this way
the breast wheel makes the most of the fall available as
in the overshot and attempts to use the force of the
moving water as in the undershot. In all types, by making
the diameter of the wheel as large as possible, taking into
consideration other demands by the machinery or building,
the maximum leverage and hence maximum effectiveness
of the water power could be obtained. In the region of
low relief described in this work, the greatest diameter
of which we know was one of 17 ft. at Bustleholme,
though this scarcely compares with the more than 40 ft.
of Darby's wheel at Coalbrookdale, or the 72 ft. of the
wheel at Laxey in the Isle of Man. Another way of
making the greatest use of the available water was to
use two or more wheels at the same mill. There were
two wheels at West Bromwich Old Forge in 1792 and
no less than five at Wednesbury Forge in 1889. We do not
know whether these wheels worked in tandem or side by
side.

The area drained by the Upper Tame and its very small
tributary streams is one of low relief and gentle gradients,

a sharp contrast to the Stour valley on the western side of the watershed. It has been argued that this led to a concentration of mills in the Stour valley to the neglect of the Tame, but further investigation shows that this was not so, for more than 40 such mills can be traced after the end of the 16th century. Early water mills used very little power. 'Such water mills were very small, generating perhaps the same horse power as a small car today, and were driven by streams which now look as though they could hardly propel a minnow, so clogged have they become with rushes and weeds. Nearly all rivers were originally much wider than they are today.'[1] It cannot be denied that the Tame did not provide a promising area, for it has a fall of no more than 300 ft. in 20 miles and an average gradient of 1 in 475 between the 500-ft. and 300-ft. contours which cover most of the area under discussion. There are very few local irregularities of profile or minor 'nick-points' to provide a temporarily increased gradient. Only two small tributary valleys, the one at Sandwell and the other at the Hobnail brook, yielded even slightly suitable natural sites for the construction of a dam and pool. Nevertheless, a dam was necessary for most of the mills to provide storage against times of low water on the river which probably never carried much at the best of times. Some writers claim that the Tame declined in volume in the late 18th and early 19th centuries due to mine flooding and diversion to canals. I suggest that not too much emphasis should be placed on these points, as the loss of water to a mine could only be a temporary effect, the constant efforts being made to pump out and drain the mines being unavailing in the end. The building of the canals certainly diverted parts of the Tame in the Oldbury area and headstreams were tapped to provide water for the Summit levels, but, every time a boat passed through the locks, water moved down towards the lower pounds where it escaped over the safety weirs to rejoin the normal drainage. The fact that so large a part of the area is now urbanised with resultant diminished soak-away and

increased run-off, and also that the South Staffordshire
Waterworks Company pumps vast quantities of water
into the district today, means that the river has to cope
with a much greater volume than ever in its earlier
days. To create a mill pool in the more level parts, it
was usual to raise an earth bank around a field. In some
cases this must have been a considerable task. The pool
at West Bromwich Old Forge covered 14½ acres and
was bounded on three sides by a bank roughly 6ft.
high and 30ft. through it! Of necessity such pools were
quite shallow. They were usually fed by a mill lade,
often of considerable length. Such a lade, on leaving the
main stream at a weir, would be made to follow fairly
closely the contour along the slope in order to attain
any head of water by the time the mill was reached.
Frequently this involved a great length of excavation.
The lade at the above forge was nearly a mile in length,
yet it only provided a head of water of four to four and a
half feet at the wheel. Walsall New Mills had a lade over
a mile long, while the Wednesbury Forge had two, from
different sources, each of a similar length. For some of
the smaller mills, a short lade with no pool seemed to
suffice. Only in the most favourable positions, as at
Sandwell and Hateley, was it possible to dam the stream
itself and avoid the construction of a race. In these cases
the mill was situated at the outflow from the mill-pool.
Occasionally two mills shared one lade, as in the case of
the Peck Mill and Wednesbury Forge; a system that
inevitably led to disputes. In general it may be said that,
in this area, the siting of a mill bore little relation to
physical environment but was rather a reflection of the
ownership of the land.

Prior to the advent of the water mill, man had had
to rely on the strength of his domestic animals to
supplement his own muscular efforts. He had no means
of harnessing the powers of nature, until, reputedly, the
Romans introduced the invention to this country. We
do not know when the first mill was erected in the
Midlands, but certainly a few were in operation in this

area in late Saxon times. Our first definite information comes from the Domesday Book from which source we learn that at the end of the 11th century there were mills at Pirrie (Perry Barr), Handsworth, Wednesbury and Rushall, with another on an unspecified site in the 13 berewicks of the Bishop of Chester, which included Tipton, Smethwick and Harborne. Compared with mills in other parts of the country these were small and considered of little value. Wednesbury and Handsworth were assessed at 2s. each, Pirrie at 16d., and Rushall at 4d., compared with 10s. at Brailes in Warwickshire. The number and value is a reflection of the sparsity of population, less than two per square mile^2 and the low level of agriculture in the area at the time. These corn mills were manorial property and an important source of revenue to the owner. Hence 'mill suit' was rigorously enforced on the inhabitants of the manor and the construction of rival mills strongly opposed. One may only conjecture as to the practices employed by the inhabitants of manors such as West Bromwich and Bilston which had no manorial corn mill at that time. Such valuable assets were assiduously acquired by the Church whenever opportunity presented. About 1180, William de Offney, lord of the manor of West Bromwich, included the mill at Grete when he endowed the Benedictine Priory of Sandwell. About 1230, William Heronville of Wednesbury bestowed the manorial mill of Wednesbury on the Abbey of Bordesley, 'for the good of his immortal soul'. This latter was the cause of protracted legal action between the Hillary and Heronville families from 1287 to 1352 over the matter of mill-suit. On the other hand the burgesses of Walsall purchased exemption from suit in 1197 from William Ruffus, the then holder of the manor.

Apart from the grinding of corn, the water mill during the Middle Ages came to be used for a variety of purposes connected with the daily life of the local people rather than an incipient manufacturing industry to supply the wants of other areas. There are examples of leather-dressing, oil seed crushing, a saw-mill and the pumping of water at Hamstead in the 17th century. Two 'Walkmills', for the fulling of cloth, made their appearance in the 15th to 17th centuries, the one in Walsall and the other on the Wednesbury–West Bromwich boundary. A blade-mill for the grinding and sharpening of edge tools existed at Bromford before the end of the 16th century. All of these mills were associated with the produce and needs of the locality and so tended to be fixtures over considerable periods.

In addition to these were the 'bloom-smithies'. These were essentially open charcoal-burning hearths on which iron ore was heated before being hammered on an anvil. Repetitions of the process drove out impurities as scale, leaving a mass of iron which the smith or 'bloomer' hammered into a 'bloom' or small ingot which was sold to other smiths for fashioning into whatever finished product was required. In its earliest form the bloom-smithy was a small establishment needing no more power than the human muscle to wield the hammer or work the bellows for the hearth. As such it tended to be mobile, being found near the charcoal-burning in woods or forests, since greater quantities of charcoal were needed than of ore. Later they were sited by streams, the water power being harnessed to operate both the bellows and the 'trip-hammer', which could, of course, be much larger and heavier than the earlier manually-used hammers. Apart from numerous small smithies, some of which were powered by water and which vanished without trace, there were in this area two water-powered bloom-smithies which existed from the early 14th century till well into the 17th century, the one at Bescot, and the other at Bloomfield on the Dudley-Tipton border.

By the end of the 16th and the early 17th centuries, the bloom-smithies were becoming obsolete with the advancement of iron technology. The 'blast furnace' was introduced, producing molten pig iron, which was then worked in forges, resembling the bloom-smithy, into billets and bars. These in turn were rolled into sheets or cut into rods at a slitting-mill, as the basic material for the nailing and other light smithy work.

The early blast furnace, working on cold blast and open to the skies above, was extremely wasteful of fuel. A good example of one may still be seen preserved in the museum at Coalbrookdale. They had changed little in a century other than size, when in 1686 Dr. Plot wrote:[3]

> the hearth of the furnace into which the ore and coal fall is ordinarily built square, the sides descending obliquely and drawing near to one another towards the bottom, like the Hopper of a Mill. Where these oblique walls terminate, which they call the boshes, there are pined four other stones but these are commonly set perpendicular and reach to the bottom stone making a perpendicular square that receives the Metall . . . the bellows . . . have usually their entrance into the furnace between the bottom of the Hopper or boshes and the bottom stone.

He also gives detailed description of the working of the furnace:[4]

> When they have gotten their ore before it is fit for the furnace they burn or calcine it upon the open ground, with small charcoal, wood or seacole, to make it break into small pieces, which will be done in three dayes, and this they call annealing it or fiting it for the furnace. In the meanwhile they also heat their furnace for a weeks time with charcoal without blowing it, which they call seasoning it, and then they bring the Ore to the furnace thus prepared and throw it in with the charcoal in baskets, a basket of Ore and then a basket of coal, where by two vast pairs of bellows placed behind the furnace are compress'd alternatly by a large wheel turned by water, the fire is made so intense, that after three days time the metal will begin to run, still after increasing till at length in fourteenights time they can run a Sow and Pigs once in 12 hours, which they doe in a bed of sand before the mouth of the furnace. . . . when it begins to blacken on the top and the red to goe off, they break the Sow and Piggs off from one another . . . whereas if let alone till they are quite cold, they will either not break at all or not without difficulty.

Although the blast furnace appears to have been introduced into Staffordshire during the second half of the

16th century,[5] it is doubtful if one was built on the Upper Tame above Perry before 1600. Shortly after that date two were constructed, one at West Bromwich Old Forge and the other at Rushall. The former had a short life of some 30 or 40 years, but the latter existed for nearly 200 years. Neither of them contributed much to the growing industry for most of the pig iron used in this area originated at the Hales, Trescot Grange or Aston furnaces.

The next process was the treatment of the pig iron. This is well described by Plot as follows:[6]

> From the Furnaces they bring the Sows and Pigs of Iron when broken asunder, and into lengths, to the Forges, which are of two sorts, but commonly standing together under one roof; one whereof they call the Finery, the other the Chafery; they are both of them open hearths, upon which they place great heaps of coal, which are blown by bellows like to those of the Furnaces, and compressed the same way, but nothing near so large. In these two forges they give the sow and piggs several heats before they are perfectly wrought into barrs. First in the Finery they are melted down thin as lead, where the Metall in an hour thickens by degrees into a lump or mass, which they call a loop, this they then bring to the great Hammer raised by the motion of a water wheel, and first beat it into a thick square which they call a half-bloom. Then they put it into the Finery again for an hour and then bring it again to the same Hammer, where they work it into a bloom, which is a square barr in the middle and two square knobs at the ends, one much less than the other, the smaller being call'd the Ancony end and the greater the Mocket head. And this is all they doe at the Finery. Then the Ancony end is brought to the Chafery, where after it has been heated for a quarter of an hour it is also brought to the Hammer, and there beat quite out to a bar, first at that end and after that, the Mocket head is brought also to the Chafery, which being thick requires two heats, before it can be wrought under the Hammer, into bars of such shapes and sizes as they think fittest for Sale.

From the late 16th century a number of forges sprang up in our area, West Bromwich, Wednesbury, Hateley, and later, Wednesbury Bridge, Golds Hill, Goscote, Horsley, Friar Park and Dunkirk.

A considerable amount of the iron forged in South Staffordshire was destined to supply the nail industry. 'For this purpose, the iron passed through the slitting mill, an interesting early example of mechanical manipulation. The bars, first hammered to a suitable size, were passed between a pair of plain rolls to reduce them to a strip, and then between two rolls with collars intersecting. This cut the strip into several smaller strips or "slit-rods" ready for use in the nailer's forge'.[7] Richard Foley is accredited with introducing the slitting-mill to the Midlands. He erected one at Hyde, near Stourbridge, in 1628. There was only one such mill, until Moore's Mill, Tipton, was converted towards the end of the 18th century, the Bustleholme Rod Mill, on the upper part of the Tame and that had almost certainly been converted to that purpose before Thomas Foley obtained the lease in 1650. This was a quite important establishment locally for it absorbed almost the complete output of the West Bromwich and Wednesbury Forges and much from the Little Aston Forge. Nevertheless, it did not cope with the growing demands of a growing Black Country, and additional supplies came from both Hyde and the Rugeley slitting-mill.

While these were the principal uses of the water mills to the iron industry it would be wrong to omit reference to others. Bustleholme was used as a 'rolling-mill' about 1820 as was Wednesbury Forge about 1705; 'blade-mills' were to be found at Bromford, *c.* 1570, and at Bustleholme, *c.* 1570, and again *c.* 1815. 'Wire mills' existed at Bromford, *c.* 1780, and at Grete, *c.* 1835. Other, less usual uses, of the water mill were the making of saws, *c.* 1725, and the grinding of gun-barrels, *c.* 1795, both at Wednesbury Forge.

Though there was a great development of activity in the use of water mills for the iron industry during the last two or three decades of the 16th century (West Bromwich Forge, Bustleholme, Hateley, Wednesbury Forge, Bromford and Oldbury, all date from that time) yet it is interesting that some resisted the change for so long.

'The Mill', at Izons, did not again become part of that industry until 1783 (after some 150 years), and at that time ceased to use water power. The Dunkirk remained a corn mill until 1835 when it became 'Spencer's Trip-hammer Mill'. Some, such as Hamstead, Walsall Old Mill, and Walsall New Mills remained faithful to the grinding of corn throughout their centuries of existence. It is interesting to note that Bustleholme, despite its varied industrial activity, never abandoned its agricultural association, always retaining a corn mill or oil mill under the same roof.

There were limits to the power that the Tame could provide and ways were sought to overcome the problem. About 1760 Sparrow's Forge was powered by a 'horse-mill'. Increasingly during the previous century corn-milling had been taken over by windmills, which, how-ever, were not powerful enough or reliable enough to be of use to the iron industry. The decline of the water-powered iron-mill was soon to come. The increased traffic in iron and coal, which was rendering the roads of South Staffordshire almost impassable at times, led to Brindley's activities in canal building from 1765. The Birmingham to Wednesbury Canal affected all the mills between, in particular those at Oldbury, Bromford, Dun-kirk, Grete, Toll End and Wednesbury Bridge, some more than others, but none was immediately put com-pletely out of action. The final blow was undoubtedly the invention of the steam-engine towards the end of the century. Without it, the pumping and winding at pits, the blowing of the later and larger blast furnaces, the turning of heavier machinery, the coming of the railways, all things necessary to the further development of the Black Country could not have come about, but it spelled death to the water mill. Some, such as Izons, abandoned water power early on, but for others it was a lingering death. A few compromised: Elwells at Wednes-bury Forge were still using water power alongside a steam-engine as late as 1889. Moore's Mill added steam to its waterwheels about 1795, while Horseley combined the two for many years. A few never fell to steam: Hamstead, West Bromwich Forge, Walsall New Mills, and Bustleholme, and as water corn mills struggled on well into this century. The sites on the higher parts of the river and tributaries, where there was even less power, with the exception of Wednesbury Forge, were all abandoned by mid-century or soon after, or were converted to foundries.

NOTES

1. W. G. Hoskins, *The Making of the English Landscape* (1955), p. 65.

2. R. H. Kinvig, 'The Birmingham District in Domesday Times'. in M. J. Wise, ed., *Birmingham and its Regional Setting* (1950), p. 131. Hereafter the title of this book is abbreviated to *B.R.S.*

3. R. Plot, *Natural History of Staffordshire* (1686), Ch. 4, para. 23.

4. *Ibid.*, Ch. 4, para. 22.

5. R. A. Pelham, 'The Growth of Settlement and Industry, *c.* 1100-1700' in *B.R.S.*, p. 147.

6. R. Plot, *op. cit.*, Ch. 4, para 24.

7. W. K. V. Gale, 'Development of Industrial Technology in the Black Country 1700-1900' in *B.R.S.*, p. 196.

PART THREE

I

HOLFORD MILL

The Holford Mill (O.S. 077917), on the right bank of the river Tame, was the lowest mill to be found on that stream before it crossed the boundary from Staffordshire into Warwickshire. In 1358, John de Botetourt, holder of the manor of Handsworth, granted permission to Roger de Wyrley, his tenant, to construct a fulling-mill with the necessary leat and sluices on what is believed to be the Holford site.

The fulling-mill does not appear to have survived the 16th century on the Upper Tame and this one is certainly no exception. The inquisition post mortem held at the death of Lady Anne St. Leger in 1533, showed that she died seized of the manor of Handsworth, which included 'a water mill and an iron mill called a hammer-mill'. The water mill would be the manorial corn mill. The hammer-mill seems to have replaced the earlier fulling-mill.

In 1549 Sir John St. Leger made inquisition on the death of William Cokes, his tenant, who died seized of the 'messuage here called Bayshall, together with, *inter alia*, 'a water mill and an iron mill called a hammer-mill, held of the said John St. Leger, knt. as of his manor of Honnisworth, by the service of 1/30th part of a knight's fee and 15s. 8d. rent'.[1]

Another inquisition of 1562 showed that 'William Wirley, Esq., died Feb. 24th. 4. Eliz. seized of Hondisworth Manor or capital messuage called Wyrley's hall and another messuage, called Hallford held of Robert Stanford Esq. by fealty' together with two water mills with a pool, moor and fishery on the Tame.[2] He also held a moiety of the manors of Perry Barr, Hamstead and Oscote, which included four water mills called Blade Mills. This suggests that he probably held Hamstead, Perry Barr, and Holford Mills together with three mills on the Holbrook.

Another elaboration on the manor of Handsworth and some account of the families connected with it, particularly the Botetourts, St. Legers and Wyrleys, will be found in the chapter dealing with the Hamstead Mill. The Stanfords and later the Goughs were holders of a moiety of the manor of Perry Barr.

In 1591, 'Humfry' Wyrley of Hamstead, son of John and grandson of Thomas and Dorothy Wyrley, married Katherin Holte. In the marriage settlement there is reference to 'all that iron Myll called or known by the name of the hamer myll in holford' and also 'one halfe af all that Corne Mill called Perry Mill'.[3] His father John died in 1596 and the inquisition post mortem mentioned the same properties.[4]

We have no proof that the Holford Mill was one of the number of local ironworks involved in the rioting in 1597.[5] If it was, then it must have been the 'iron forge. in Handsworth, operated by Thomas Parkes of Wednesbury as sub-tenant, which was sacked on 14 July.

The above-mentioned Humphrey Wyrley, by that time a widower, re-married in 1615 one, Knightley Wyrley (a cousin?); The marriage settlement is slightly different from the earlier one of 1591.[6] This one refers to 'the Iron mylle or hammermylle with appurtainances and the grounde to the same mylle in Hollford', 'and also all that Blade Mylle comonly called the Garrette blade mylle . . . in Perry Barre'. This blade-mill was probably on the upper part of the Holbrook.

Hackwood, without quoting his source, refers to a fine levied by Humphrey Wyrley in 1626 in favour of his

son John Wyrley and John Parkhouse on property which
included 10 mills, some being in this area.[7]

Sir John Wyrley of Hamstead Hall in 1654 leased to
William Edwards of 'Derringtend' in Aston (grinder), and
John Crooley of Birmingham (grinder), the blade-mill
at Holford. It was described as being of two 'bayes' on
the river near Holford.[8] Included was the 'use of the ways,
passages and privileges belonging thereto when the same
was a furnace or Ironworks and in the holding of Thomas
Foley'. This document raises several questions. When
and for how long had Thomas Foley held it? In general,
he did not take over any of the Upper Tame mills,
usually from his father Richard, before 1650. Was this a
separate venture? Why such a short tenure when the
Foley family continued to hold other sites until almost
the end of the century? Was this really a furnace at
Holford? If so, it is the only reference that we have to
such on this site. Possibly the answer is that it was not
at Holford, but near Holford, perhaps the lowest site on
the Holbrook. This would solve some of the questions.

Even if the above was not the Holford Mill, it is probable
that it was about this time that the old hammer-mill was
converted to a blade-mill. We have no records of it for the
next hundred or so years until we find that John Dalloway
was the tenant in 1794.[9]

It is strange that this mill does not appear on Yates's
Maps of Staffordshire, 1769-98, yet, writing in 1798,
Shaw describes it as 'a blade mill belonging to Messrs.
Wooley & Co., Birmingham, for the purpose of grinding
sword blades'.[10] This firm continued there as grinders for
at least another decade. By 1815 it had been taken over
by Thomas Wilmore, 'manufacturer of rolled, plated,
gilding and dipping metal, wires etc.'.[11]

From that time on there were a number of changes
in tenancy. The Handsworth Tithe Award named Thomas
Clows as tenant in 1839.[12] James Turner, gun-barrel
manufacturer, was named as occupant in 1855[13] and again
in 1863, according to *Cornish's Corporation Directory.*

The National Arms and Ammunition Company had taken over by 1875[14] and this in turn was absorbed by the Imperial Chemical Industries.

NOTES

1. Stebbing Shaw, *Natural History of Staffordshire* (1798), vol. 1, p. 110
2. *Ibid.*
3. Birmingham Reference Library, 276768.
4. Stebbing Shaw, *op. cit.*, p. 111.
5. *Staffordshire Quarter Session Rolls* (1597), (*Staffordshire Historical Collection* [1932], p. 300). Hereafter *Staffordshire Historical Collection* will be abbreviated to *S.H.C.*
6. Birmingham Reference Library, 276767.
7. F. W. Hackwood, *History of West Bromwich* (1895), p. 49.
8. Birmingham Reference Library, 252214.
9. *Ibid.*, 610704.
10. Stebbing Shaw, *op. cit.*, vol. 1, p. 117.
11. *Wrightson's Triennial Directory* (1815).
12. Birmingham Reference Library, 299997.
13. *White's Directory of Birmingham* (1855).
14. *Ibid.* (1875).

II

THE HOLBROOK MILLS

The Holbrook, a left-bank tributary of the Tame, rises in Great Barr and flows southward through Perry Barr to join the main stream between Perry Barr Mill and Holford. The lowest mile was for long a favourite site for mills. Unfortunately it is usually impossible to locate the exact position of a particular mill, for they were often demolished, rebuilt or changed their uses. Consequently it will be necessary to mass all information together and hope that some picture emerges.

The earliest reference that we have in 1543, is to a bloom-smithy in Handsworth, operated by one Henry Grove.[1] In view of the fact that we have not located such an establishment on the right bank of the river, i.e., in Handsworth, and in view of the next item, we suggest that it must have been on the Holbrook. In the following year, 1544, William Wyrley, of Handsworth, engaged Henry Grove, an 'iron-branner' of Perry Barr, to work for one year in his 'Branne-Smithy' in Perry Barr, known as Perry Smithy. We learn that Perry Smithy was burnt down by the negligence of the said Henry[2] but was reconstructed. William Wyrley at this time held a moiety of Perry Barr from the Stanford family.

This was a period of growth in the iron industry and Hackwood informs us that there were four blade-mills in 1560.[3] When William Wyrley died in 1562, the inquisition post mortem showed that he held two water corn mills and four blade-mills, the latter almost certainly on the Holbrook.[4] It will be noted that there is no mention of the 'branne-smithy' (bloom-smithy). It may have been a period when the smithy was not operating, for, in any case, they were soon to be replaced by the hopper-type open charcoal furnace. In 1597, his son, Humphrey Wyrley, possessed the moiety of a 'smithy or furnace' in Perry Barr.[5] At the same time the blade-mill was proliferating, for from the same document we learn of the Garrett blade-mill which we believe to have been sited further upstream.

Considerable competition—or was it antagonism?—rose between the operators of the iron mills of this area in this year and culminated in July in a series of attacks on each others premises.[6] The first attack was on 8 July on the mill mentioned above. It was described as a 'furnace mill for the making of iron' owned jointly by Humphrey and Robert Stamforde and farmed, i.e., tenant-operated by William Whorwood of Sandwell (*q.v.*), who was expelled from the mill. The attack was led by Thomas Parkes, ironmaster of Wednesbury (*q.v.*), who worked a number of other establishments including West Bromwich Old Forge (*q.v.*). On 14 July, the Whorwood faction made no less than four retaliatory attacks. One was on a 'furnace for melting and casting iron' in Perry Barr, operated by Parkes. On the 18th, Edward Ashmore, employee of Parkes, returned to the fray at the Perry Barr 'mill for making iron' worked by Whorwood. This may have been a second attack on the same mill. From these cases we can judge that there were two furnaces at that date on the Holbrook. What was the cause of these affrays? Probably insufficient water power for two such establishments so close together. We shall never know for we do not have the depositions of the cases.

A few entries in the Handsworth parish registers give some indication of the work being carried on. In 1599 William Hopkins was a 'finer' and in 1613 Blithe Dickinson was working at a forge. One or both of these could have been at Holford or at a Holbrook forge. In 1602 John Lapwicke was 'filler at Pury furnace' and Blasius Vyntam, a 'finer at Purye Forge'. The latter was a finer for Whorwood at Wednesbury Forge, five years previously.

The marriage settlement of Humphrey Wyrley in 1615 (chapter I) contains reference to 'all that Blade Mylle comonle called Garrette blade mylle in Perry Barre'.[7] This is the last date that we have found for that particular mill.

A different use was soon to be found for a mill on the Holbrook. In 1648, Sir John Wyrley leased to Thomas Blakemore of Perry Barr a pasture near to a paper mill recently erected by his father, Humphrey Wyrley.[8] Paper mills were to be a feature of this area for many years to come.

We are informed by Hackwood without a quoted source of information, that in 1654 Thomas Foley occupied a blade-mill above Perry Bridge.[9] We are tempted to wonder whether this is not a confusion of the reference to the Wyrley lease of 1654 to Edwards and Crooley which refers to 'a furnace or ironworks in the holding of Thomas Foley' (*see* chapter I).[10] It would seem reasonably certain that the latter was on the Holbrook and had ceased to operate by this date.

It was probably this same blade-mill of which the lease was conveyed by Humphrey Wyrley II of Hamstead Hall, to John Doley in 1691.[11] At the time Samuel Porter was the occupant. The mill, on the Holbrook, was described as being on the road from Perry Hall to Sutton Coldfield, i.e., close to Church Road, Perry Barr.

Further light is thrown on the paper-making industry when in 1680, Sir John Wyrley leased to Samuel Jerrom, two paper mills on Perry Brook.[12] The assumption is that one of them was the paper mill referred to in 1648.

So we find, in the second half of the 17th century, four mills on the Holbrook, two paper mills and two blade-mills, all belonging to the Wyrley family. As might have been expected the furnaces had gone.

The 18th century provides little information on these mills, though it is obvious that the number and use continued to change. It is stated that there were four mills on the Holbrook in 1733.[13]

It may be well at this point to locate the sites on this brook, known to have been used. Site 1 (069923) was on the north side of Church Lane, Perry Barr, 250yds. north-west of the church. Site 2 (069924) was about 170yds. north of site 1, and on the stream on the east side of the No. 1 pool. Site 3 (067927) was half a mile north-north-west of No. 2, the pool having been cut at a later date by the construction of the canal. Site 4 (067931) was about 350yds. further north, on the north side of Thornbridge Avenue near to the Hathersage Road junction. Two hundred yards further north still, between Hathersage Road and Castleton Road was site 5 (068934). The pool for this site was the confluence of the Barr Brook, the course of which was altered at the building of the estate, and the Oscott brook, now in a conduit. There was another mill in Old Oscott, on the brook of that name (074942).

In 1788, Samuel Harvey, a sword-cutler, holder of the leases of two of these mills, was bankrupt and his assignees sold the leases of these two blade-mills to Thomas Archer, button-maker, and James Woolley, sword-cutler, respectively. The first sale, on 16 December, to Archer for £600 referred to a mill used as a blade-mill and dwelling-house in Perry Barr.[14] The second, on 20 December, to James Woolley of Birmingham for £320 was for Perry blade-mill.[15] It will be seen that it is not possible to positively identify these two mills, though from other evidence it seems probable that the Woolley (Perry Barr blade-mill) was on the No. 1. site. However this does not fully accord with the suggestion,[16] that the mill on this site was owned by John Gough, whose tenant was George Birch, and sub-tenants William Bayliss (1775-81) and Thomas Archer (1781-91). This source further states that this mill had been formerly a blade-mill, then a paper mill, and at the end of the century was grinding gun-barrels.

A map of Perry Barr by Botham in 1794 shows the sites 1, 4 and 5 to be occupied, the pool without buildings on site 3 and the remains of a pool on the Oscott site.[17]

The Enclosure Award for Perry Barr in 1814 shows that the lowest mill, the old Perry Barr blade-mill, had become a wire-mill,[18] but four years later in 1818 there was a suggestion that it had become a paper mill, occupied by John Benson,[19] though in view of the 1843 Handsworth Tithe Award map, it is more than likely that Benson occupied another mill further up the brook. This award is quite explicit.[20] The old Perry Barr Mill, No. 1, was a paper mill owned by Joseph Webster and occupied by William Brindley. The adjacent mill, No. 2, was the flour mill of John Gough. No. 3 site showed the large rectangular pool with no buildings. The sites Nos. 4 and 5 were both owned by Wyrley Birch, a descendant of the Wyrley family of 300 years earlier, the lower being a wire-mill occupied by William Bedson and the upper a rolling-mill. There was no mill here in the hands of a Benson, but the administrators of the estate of William Benson held a fish pool. This appears significant. The old Oscott site was owned by Wyrley Birch and occupied by Thomas Loynes. The pool still existed but no mill.

As was usual the corn mill changed hands frequently. In 1818 it was worked by Charles Gallimore.[21] William Allen was the miller at Paper Mill End, Perry Barr in 1834[22] and William Hollister in 1855.[23]

By 1863, the Gough property had passed into the hands of the Calthorpe Estates. A map of these estates in Perry Barr, shows that the canal had been constructed close to the No. 3 site and had considerably reduced the area of the pool.[24] The mills at the sites 1, 2, 4 and 5 still existed though there was no indication of their use at that date, which was very late for iron work.

The first edition of the 6in. O.S. map of 1884 shows that all the mills had gone, though traces remained. The reduced pool close to the canal has become the reservoir and boating pool in the Perry Park. The one-time rolling-mill buildings and a reduced pool were marked on both the second (1906) and third (1921) editions of the 1in. O.S. map, but the area has since been built over.

NOTES

1. P.R.O., C 1/1011/63.
2. P.R.O., C 1/1170/101.
3. F. W. Hackwood, *Handsworth, Old and New* (1908), p. 16.
4. Stebbing Shaw, *op. cit.*, vol. 1, p. 110
5. B. M., Add. Ch., 41830.
6. *Staffordshire Quarter Session Rolls* (1597), (*S.H.C.*, 1932, pp. 297-299.
7. Birmingham Reference Library, 276767.
8. *Ibid.*, 181865.
9. F. W. Hackwood, *Wednesbury Workshops* (1889), p. 50.
10. Birmingham Reference Library, 252214.
11. *Ibid.*, 181860.
12. *Ibid.*, 181858.
13. *Ibid.*, 157214.
14. *Ibid.*, 330472.
15. *Ibid.*, 329086.
16. *Ibid.*, 157214.
17. *Ibid.*, 601705.
18. *Perry Barr Inclosure Award* (1814), Stafford County Record Office.
19. *Parson and Bradshaw Directory* (1818).
20. Birmingham Reference Library, 299997.
21. *Parson and Bradshaw Directory* (1818).
22. *White's Directory of Staffordshire* (1834).
23. *White's Directory of Birmingham* (1855).
24. Birmingham Reference Library, 432794.

III

GREAT BARR MILL

The Great Barr Mill (056944) was situated just inside the southern boundary of the Great Barr Hall, for long the home of the Scott family. Any documentary evidence as to the age or use of this mill may exist in the family archives, but such have not been available. It is most probable that it was an estate corn mill or a saw mill.

It was first marked on the W. Yates's *Map of Staffordshire* (1775), and continued on the later editions. By 1834 as shown on the first edition 1in. O.S. map, the mill buildings and a very small pool existed, but immediately above the pool the stream had been dammed to create a large ornamental lake. It would appear that the mill ceased to be used during Victorian times, for by 1909 the site of the mill pool was occupied by a plantation.[1] The artificial lakes are still to be seen in the grounds of what is now a mental hospital.

NOTE

1. 1in. O.S. map, 2nd edition (1909).

IV

PERRY HALL MILL

The Perry Mill (067912), close to the site of the old Perry Barr Hall, was on the left bank or Perry Barr side of the Tame, situated on a short leat cut across the great curve of the stream at that point. It was the manorial mill of that manor.

This is a mill site of great antiquity, for in the Domesday record we find that Drogo held of William fitz Ansculf, his overlord at Dudley, three hides in Pirio, and 'ibi molin de xvi den.' like the other mills on the Upper Tame at that time, a small one of little value, 16d.

Nothing more is recorded of this mill for nearly 500 years, though there can be little doubt that it remained the manorial corn mill throughout that time. By the mid-16th century it appears that the Stanford family had parted with some of the properties and rights of the Perry Barr manor. In 1562, an inquisition post mortem showed that William Wyrley died seised of the manor of Handsworth and the moiety of the manors of Perry Barr, Hamstead and Oscote.[1] Since the property included two water mills (i.e., corn mills) and four blade-mills in this area it is arguable that Perry Barr Corn Mill was one of them.

In view of the above, one is tempted to question the meaning of the statement 'in 1576 one half of Perry Mill was granted to Thomas Wyrley by John Ward'.[2] It is possible that the moiety was only held on lease, both by William and son Thomas.

We learn that Thomas Smith was the miller at Perry Barr in 1602.[3] The mill at that time was held in moiety by Humphrey Wyrley, grandson of the above Thomas. Among the properties enumerated in the marriage settlement of this Humphrey Wyrley[4] in 1592 was 'one halfe of all that Corne Mylle called Perry Myll'. The inquisition held at the death of his father John, in 1596, lists the same properties in almost identical terms.[5]

In 1632, Hymphrey Wyrley leased to John Curtler, miller, of Walsall 'that moietes or one halfe parte of the Water Mylle called Perry Mylle scituate and being in Perry Barre'.[6] It was stipulated as a condition of lease that Curtler should not carry corn to the mill other than from his house at Walsall or his mills at Wednesbury. This clause was obviously inserted to protect the milling trade at the other corn mills of the district, Hamstead, which also belonged to the Wyrleys. It is probable that the Wednesbury Mills referred to were windmills situated near to the church on Wednesbury hill. This lease was for 11 years at an annual rental of £6.

The mill could not have survived long after the termination of the Curtler lease for in 1650 William Spencer took the lease for 25 years at an annual rental of £6 of 'all that Milplace whereupon formerly stood a Corne Mill situate and being in Perry Barre by the name of Perry Mill'.[7] The conditional clauses of the lease permitted Spencer to restore the sluices, etc., and build whatever type of mill he wished other than corn or paper mills. The embargo on the paper mills was for a similar reason to that on the corn mill; Wyrley had recently built such on the Holbrook. We cannot learn what type of mill Spencer did construct: another blade- or rolling-mill?

After a century, lacking in information, we find the mill marked on Yates's map of 1769, and again on the Botham map of 1794.[8]

By the beginning of the 19th century the mill had reverted to the grinding of corn. In 1818 Charles Gallimore was the miller.[9] Samuel Elwell carried on the same business from at least 1834 to 1843.[10] By 1851, John Wilcox occupied the mill,[11] and four years later William Hollister had taken it over.[12]

There is no indication that the mill was still in use in 1887.[13] We are told that the buildings were demolished in the 1890s and a model farm built on the site.[14] Hackwood stated that the dried channel of the leat was still to be seen in 1908.[15]

NOTES

1. Stebbing Shaw, *op. cit.*, vol. 1, p. 110.

2. K. E. Marsh, unpublished MS., Extramural Dept., Birmingham University.

3. Birmingham Reference Library, 661029.

4. *Ibid.*, 276768.

5. Stebbing Shaw, *op. cit.*, vol. 1, p. 111.

6. F. W. Hackwood, *Handsworth, Old and New* (1908), p. 22.

7. Birmingham Reference Library, 181855.

8. *Ibid.*, 601705.

9. *Parson and Bradshaw Directory* (1818).

10. *White's Directory of Staffordshire* (1834); Perry Barr Tithe Award, 1834; Handsworth Tithe Apportionment, 1843, Birmingham Reference Library, 299997.

11. *White's History of Staffordshire and Lichfield* (1851).

12. *White's Directory of Birmingham* (1855).

13. 6in. O.S. map, 1st edition, 1887.

14. V.C.H., *Warws.*, vol. 7 (1964), p. 255.

15. F. W. Hackwood, *Handsworth, Old and New* (1908), p. 21.

V

HAMSTEAD MILL

One of the oldest mills on the Upper Tame was undoubtedly Hamstead Mill (049927). Here the normally broad valley is constricted by the approach of a spur on either side, which was used by the Old Walsall Road from Birmingham. At this point, no doubt, the velocity of the stream was increased and it was easier to construct a short leat or a dam. At various times the one or the other was used, sometimes the leat forming the head-race direct and at others a pool was constructed alongside the river separated from it by an earth bank about 10 or 12ft. high and fed by a short leat from further up stream. In this case the mill was situated on the bank, between pool and river.

As usual, we have no idea of the original date of foundation but we do know that it was extremely early. It appears to have been part of the estate held by the Saxon Ailwerd at the time of Edward the Confessor. At the Domesday census, as part of the Handsworth manor, it was held by Drogo, from his overlord William fitz Ansculf. Fitz Ansculf, one of the great landowners of Norman England, controlled his Staffordshire lands, which included the manors of West Bromwich, Handsworth, Perry Barr, Great and Little Barr, Rushall, Bradley, and Ettingshall, from his seat at Dudley. Already the mill was one of the more valuable in this area, being assessed at 2s. It was a corn mill then and was to remain such for the 900 years of its further existence.

In the reign of Henry II, the manor passed to Paganus de Parles in whose family it remained for nearly 150 years. William de Parles held it in the time of Henry III, of

Sir Roger de Somery, Lord of Dudley. The de Somery family were successors of fitz Ansculf.[1] William came to an untimely end, being hanged for felony. The inquisition post mortem of his property in 1279 showed that he was in receipt of a rent of 20s. per annum from the prior of Sandwell for the mill at Hamstead.[2] The property continued to be held by the de Parles from the de Somery family and some 10 years later we find John de Parles in possession. In 1291, Agnes, widow of Roger de Somery, was awarded the manor as part of her dower.[3] Two years later, Thomas de Hamstede sued William le Mouner (the miller) of Handsworth, for a mill which had been left to him by his grandfather.[4] Hackwood suggests that Thomas was of the Wyrley family. If that is so, it is the first reference to the Wyrleys who were to be so important in the district. They must have been sub-tenants of the de Parles at that time.

The next William de Parles, holder of the manor under another Roger de Somery, also came to a sudden end, being hanged in 1327 while on a journey to the Holy Land.[5] The manor then passed to the de Botecourts (Botetorts?). The Subsidy Roll of 1332 contains the names of Joanna Botetort, Robert Wyrley and William Moldun (the miller) under the heading of Handsworth.[6]

From the de Botecourts, Handsworth passed to the Boteler family and on the execution of James Boteler, Earl of Wiltshire, for treason and revolt, in 1460, it was sequestrated to the crown, being granted to the Wrottesleys in 1466. Eventually it was inherited by James, fifth Earl of Ormond. In 1533, Lady Anne St. Leger, of the Ormond family, died, seised of the manor. Included in the property was 'a water mill [i.e., corn] and an iron mill called a hammer mill'. It is probable that the corn mill was Hamstead while the iron mill was downstream at or near Perry Barr.

While the various families mentioned above were the titular holders of the manor, the Wyrleys remained resident at Hamstead, growing in possessions, power and influence with the passage of time. On the death of

William Wyrley Esq. in 1562, the inquisition post mortem showed him to be seised of Handsworth Manor, called Wirley's Hall, two water mills, pool, moor, fishing in the Tame, etc., a moiety of the manors of Perry Barr, Hamstead, and Oscote, which included 'four water-mills called blade mills'.[7]

The marriage settlement of Humfrey Wyrley of Hamstead, in 1591,[8] and the inquisition post mortem of John de Wyrley in 1596, enumerate the same property.[9]

It has been shown in the previous chapter that there was keen competition for corn-milling in the district, and the Wyrleys made efforts to protect their mill at Hamstead by restrictive covenants on other properties. In 1659, a lease by Sir John Wyrley of 'Hampsteed' Hall to William Smallwood of Hansworth, hatter, of a house and appurtenances, included the condition that Smallwood should grind all the corn and malt used in his house at 'the Mills of the said Sir John Wyrley called Hamsteed Mills'.[10]

The use of the mill for an additional purpose was described by Dr. Plot in 1686.[11] 'At Hamstead Hall there is a corn mill that pumps water up into a lofty house near it, whence all the offices of the Hall are served, the pump working as the mill wheel goes to grind the corn, much as the same manner as the water-house near the bridge at London'.

Throughout the 18th and 19th centuries the mill continued to grind corn. In 1766 Thomas Bell was the miller.[12] Yates's maps of 1775 and 1798 mark the position of the mill on a leat, but it will be noticed that the mill appears to the east of the road and not to the west as shown on later maps. This is explained by the fact that the 'Old Walsall Road' followed the line of present 'Hamstead Hall Avenue' and not that of the present 'Hamstead Hill' which had not been constructed at that time.

James Swain, the miller of 1818[13] was still working there in 1836.[14] On the 6in. O.S. map of 1889 it was marked as a 'Corn Mill'. In 1908, Harry Andrews was the miller.[15] Frank Andrews, the miller in 1920, was most probably the last to operate the mill, for by 1928 the mill was derelict and the pool, heavily silted, was reed-grown and a receptacle for rubbish deposited by children from local estates.[16] The remains were finally demolished and the dam filled by the Birmingham Corporation using it as a refuse dump in the late 1940s.

NOTES

1. *Tenure Rolls*, Hen. III.
2. *Inquisition*, 8 Edw. I (*S.H.C.*, 1911, p. 174).
3. Stebbing Shaw, *op. cit.*, vol. 1, p. 110.
4. F. W. Hackwood, *Handsworth, Old and New* (1908), p. 16.
5. Stebbing Shaw, *op. cit.*, vol. 1, p. 110.
6. *Subsidy Roll*, 1332 (*S.H.C.*, x, p. 102).
7. Stebbing Shaw, *op. cit.*, vol. 1, p. 111.
8. Birmingham Reference Library, 276768.
9. Stebbing Shaw, *op. cit.*, vol. 1, p. 111.
10. F. W. Hackwood, *Handsworth, Old and New* (1908), p. 22.
11. R. Plot, *op. cit.*, p. 337.
12. Birmingham Reference Library, 362866.
13. *Parson and Bradshaw Directory* (1818).
14. *White's Directory of Staffordshire* (1836).
15. *Kelly's Directory of Staffordshire* (1908).
16. *Kelly's Birmingham and Staffordshire Directory* (1920).

VI

SANDWELL MILL

One of the smaller and less important mills, yet one which has a life of some 600 years was the Sandwell Mill (025922), situated in the Park of that name. Throughout its uneventful history, it was associated with firstly the Priory and later with the owners of the Hall standing on that site.

It was probably first built at the end of the 12th century. It was about 1180 that Gervase Paganell, 'Domini Honoris de Dudley', confirmed the gift by his knight, William, son of Guy of Offney, holder of the manor of West Bromwich, of land and property in West Bromwich to monks of the Benedictine order.[1] This charter, remarkably explicit in its detail, describes the major area of land as around the 'hermitagium in Bromwich, juxta fontem qui dicitur Sandwell'. There is no reference to a mill on the site at that time, though a mill at Grete was included in the gift.

Once the monks had established themselves, clearing the woodland and building the earliest priory, it would not be long before they constructed a mill to grind the corn, so necessary for their own sustenance and the hospitality they were expected to dispense. The earliest actual reference to this important, if commonplace, building, was in 1291, when the 'Taxatio Ecclesiastica P. Nicholai IV, listing the temporal property of the Prior of Sandwell states 'et habet ibm. duo molend. p.ann. x.s.'.[2] These two mills were the one at Grete, already held for a hundred years, and the one owned and worked by the monks at the Priory.

It would be unreasonable to expect such a humble edifice to be recorded in many documents, and we can only assume that for the next 200 years or so it continued its tasks, undergoing repairs to its elementary machinery and even rebuilding of its timber-framed building from time to time as it became necessary. In 1526 came the suppression of the Priory, its buildings, lands and assets being granted to Cardinal Wolsey for the support of the 'College of Thomas Wolsey at Oxford' (Christ Church). The Priory was stated to include a garden, orchard, water mill, etc.[3] The buildings, described in some detail, included the church, the residential buildings of cells and dormitory, the hall which was used as a refectory, the kitchens, larder, buttery, etc., and the porter's lodge; a barn, hay-house, cattle sheds and stable, and malting kiln. 'Item, there is a water miln thacked buylded wt. good substanc' tymber, cont' in lenght xxj fote & in hede xv ffote, which was wont to goo by the water of the pools which be now dekaied & wt a little cost wold be made to goo ageyn for it hath suffic' water belongyng to it if the hedds of the pools were mendyed . . . Item, iij pools dekaied wt a sour spryng rounyng thoro theme.'[4] An inquisition, 4 October, 17 Henry VIII, into the property of John Bayley, the last Prior, quotes a similar list.[5]

After the suppression of the Priory, the property passed through several hands. Hackwood states that in 1558 it was held by the Cliffords.[6] A Final Concord dated 1569 records the transfer to Robert Whorwood, of London, by John Cortt, armiger, of the manor of Sandwell.[7] The property detailed was much as described 30 years earlier and included one water mill. Robert Whorwood was the first of five generations of that family to own the estate.

When Robert died in 1590 he was seised of the manor of Sandwell which included one water mill. The whole passed to his son, Sir William Whorwood. He, like his contemporaries, the Stanleys and Turtons locally, the Parkes of Wednesbury and the Foleys of the Stour valley,

took an active part in the developing iron industry based
on the water mills. There is no evidence that he tried to
convert the Sandwell mill to such purposes, as no doubt
the water supply was insufficient. He preferred to rent
the Perry Barr Mills of the Wyrleys, lords of the manor
of Handsworth, and there he operated a furnace, which
called for greater power. For a time he also worked
the Wednesbury Mill of the Comberfords, lords of
the manor of Wednesbury, as a forge.[8] On his death
in 1614 the same property, including the Sandwell Mill
passed to his son, Sir Thomas Whorwood, who held it
for 20 years. In his turn he was succeeded by his son,
Brome Whorwood, who took an active part in the Civil
War and died in 1654. He was followed by his son,
Thomas Brome Whorwood, who remained at Sandwell
for the rest of the century.[9]

In 1701, the Whorwoods sold the estate to William,
Baron Dartmouth, later to become the first Earl of
Dartmouth. The first four earls resided at Sandwell, but
William Walter, fifth Earl of Dartmouth, on his succession
in 1853, moved to Patsull, near Wolverhampton. From
that time until its demolition in the 1920, the Hall
was used by a variety of organisations and the land
rented out to tenant farmers. It would seem that the
mill was unlikely to have survived as a working unit
long after 1853.

The story of the mill during the Dartmouth period is a
little confused. The 1775 map of William Yates shows
and names it as a slitting-mill. The accuracy of this raises
questions. As previously stated, it is unlikely that this
mill would be sufficiently powerful to take much part in
the industry. There is no evidence at present that William,
the second earl had any interest in the industry. He took
little part in West Bromwich life but was an active peer
and member of the government. Nevertheless, the mill
stated to be 'about ½ a mile from Sandwell' about 1790
is most probably our Sandwell Mill.[10] It was described as 'a
mill for rolling and slitting iron, the property of Charles
Leonard Esq.'. This would appear to be the same

Mr. Leonard who worked the Friar Park Forge and the Bustieholme Mill (*see* chapter IX). A plan, dated 1827, in the Quarter Session records names the mill as a 'forge' but, at the same time, names the meadow to the immediate north of it as 'Slitting Mill Meadow'.[11]

The Dawson map (1816), the Furneyhough map (1819) and the first edition 1in. O.S. map (1834) all mark and name Sandwell Mill.

The census returns of 1851 reveal a change of use for at that time it was the estate saw-mill, with two adjacent cottages, one occupied by William White, sawyer. As previously stated it is conjectural as to how much longer it continued in use. The 1885 6in. O.S. map shows it as a corn mill, but by the 1889 edition it had been altered to 'saw-mill'. This is not evidence that it was still working.

With the sinking of the Jubilee Pit on the Sandwell Park Colliery Company in 1898 the mill site was buried under the spoil heap which also reduced the size of the pool. This pool, known locally as Warstone (pronounced Wosson) Pool, or Swan Pool, survives to the present day.

NOTES

1. M. Willett, *History of West Bromwich* (1882), pp. 145-6.
2. Stebbing Shaw, *op cit.*, vol. 1, p. xxi.
3. F. W. Hackwood, *History of West Bromwich* (1895), p. 26.
4. P.R.O., E 36/165, f. 128v.
5. Stebbing Shaw, *op. cit.*, vol. 2, p. 128.
6. F. W. Hackwood, *History of West Bromwich* (1895), p. 54.
7. *Final Concords,* 1569 (*S.H.C.*, xiii, p. 274).
8. *Staffordshire Quarter Session Rolls* (1597), (*S.H.C.*, 1932, pp. 298-9).
9. F. W. Hackwood, *History of West Bromwich* (1895), p. 56.
10. *Universal British Directory*, vol. 4, p. 707.
11. Staffordshire County Records Office, Q/SB, A.1838.

VII

OLD FORGE MILL

The Old Forge Mill, frequently designated West Bromwich Forge in times past, is another ancient establishment, though probably not quite so old as some would have us believe. The proximity to the old Sandwell Priory has been used as an argument that this was a monasterial foundation. Unfortunately there appears to be no evidence to support this theory and against it is the fact that the land in this area was manorial property until the early 18th century when it was bought by the Earl of Dartmouth. The Whorwood family who held the Sandwell lands for over a hundred years never possessed this property.

The mill (028927) is situated near to the point where the Tame, meandering along the particularly broad and level part of its valley, receives from the west and south, a couple of small tributary brooks draining the water from the Sandwell Park area. The site would appear to be particularly unsuitable for the construction of a mill as the valley floor has scarcely a 5-ft. difference in more than half a mile of width, and the river itself a fall of less than 20ft. in two miles. The determining factor appears to have been that this is the point at which the river left the manor, the lowest available site within the manorial lands.

Reeves suggests that it was originally built here by Walter Stanley, lord of the manor of West Bromwich from 1557 to 1615.[1] As he was but 10 years of age in 1557 it seems improbable that the mill was built before 1567 if Reeves's supposition is correct. John Izon stated that Thomas Parkes, an ironmaster of Wednesbury obtained the permission of Walter Stanley in 1585 to dig the necessary mill lade and erect a forge, furnace and cottages on this site.[2] Regretably he fails to quote the source of this information. It should be borne in mind that Walter Stanley himself purchased the Bustleholme Mill in 1594. In 1597 there arose a number of cases at the Staffordshire Quarter Sessions out of a series of raids by rival factions on ironworks in this district.[3] One of these attacks was on the iron forge of Walter Stanley, at West Bromwich, operated by Thomas Parkes. In this foray the raiders used the waggon and a team of oxen of William Whorwood to remove 'a thousand pounds of bar iron, thirty seven pieces of bar iron weighing fifteen hundred pounds, one paire of Chaferie Bellowes, two paire of ffinerie Bellowes, seven pair of tongs, three chisels, one great forge hammer' and a long list of tools. They stripped the forge. There is no mention of a furnace at the site, but since there is such mention of furnaces at other sites, it seems that the forge existed in the 1590s but not the furnace.

Five years later, in 1602, in another case before the Quarter Sessions, 'John Partridge, a tanner of Smethwicke' gave evidence that he was in a 'lane called Jane Mill' close by the 'tourning of the water ofte tymes to a newe erected forge or Ironworke'.[4] It seems probable that this is a reference to the Old Forge since the mill lade certainly ran by the site of the Joan Mill until destroyed by the construction of the motorway in 1968. It is difficult, however, to accept the term 'newe erected' if the forge had actually been in existence for seven years or more.

The incomplete Manorial Rent Roll of 1604 contains no reference to the forge but this is not evidence of its non-existence. After the death of Thomas Parkes in 1602, the business was continued by his son, Richard Parkes of Wednesbury. In 1606 he was 'fined' 4d. along with other defaulters who failed to present themselves before the West Bromwich Manorial Court. He then took the precaution of paying 1s. to excuse him of attendance for the next 12 months. In the same year, he must have tried to increase the height of the water in the dam at the Forge for he was charged that he 'raised or stopped up the watercourse at Johan mill pool tayle so that Thomas Walstead and his tenants are hindered in their entry, egress and regress with their beasts to the meadow of the same Thomas'. He was fined 4d. and warned to desist.[5] In 1609, he once more failed to appear before the Court Baron and once more he compounded for the abatement of suit for the following year.[6] The Manorial Court Roll of 1609 contains mention of 'George Rowe of the Forge'. He was presumably one of the workmen at 'the Forge' but we do not know that this was the only forge within the manor at that time. The first exact definition of the site that we have occurs in the Manorial Court Roll of 1619, when the Jury, on 'walking the bounds' defined the West Bromwich boundary as running 'by the little perle brook near to the furnace'. This would indicate that by that time there existed here the complete ironworks, consisting of the open, cold blast, charcoal-consuming furnace, to smelt the ore and produce the pig iron, and alongside, the forge or 'hammer-mill' where the re-heated pig iron was shaped into bars to be sold to the slitting-mill.

After the death of Richard Parkes, his son, Thomas Parkes, gent., of Willingsworth carried on from 1619. In that year he failed to present suit for the property.[7] By 1625 the Parkes interest terminated.

The furnace was soon in a state of disrepair, for we learn from the Manorial Rent Roll of 1626 that 'Richard Foley houldeth the fordge for ten yeares from our Ladyday, 1625, at the yearely rent of £20. Allsoe he houldeth the furnace for the same tyme payinge nothing duringe the terme of six yeares in Regard of repayring of the same And then has to pay for the four last yeares p. ann. £10'.[8] Thus the forge became part of the Foley enterprises which played such an important part in the growing iron industry of the Midlands. However, the West Bromwich Furnace could not have been one of their more profitable ventures for the Manorial Rent Roll of

1630 reveals that the rent paid by Richard Foley for the 'forge or hammer mill' was still £20 but that of the furnace had been reduced to 1s.!⁹ By 1649 there was no mention of a furnace and 'Mr. Foley' was paying a rent of £7 10s. for the forge.[10]

The names of some of the 17th-century workmen resident at the forge are to be found in the parish registers of West Bromwich and elsewhere. In 1658, Samuel, son of William Traford of the forge, was born, while in 1659, Thomas France of the forge married Hannah Brookes of Birmingham. From 1689 to 1720 there is a series of entries relating to the 'Minner' (Minor, Miner, Minns) family of that address. It is not possible to identify the tenants of the two cottages from the 1666 Hearth Tax Returns,[11] but they could well be included among the 117 West Bromwich households which were exempt.

In 1667 the empire of Thomas Foley was shared among his three surviving sons, the Stour valley properties, which included the forges at West Bromwich, Wednesbury and Little Aston and the slitting-mill at Bustleholme, becoming the province of the youngest, Philip Foley of Prestwood. From 1667 to 1672, at least, William Spencer was the manager of these three forges.[12]

On 14 September 1669 Walter Needham and Elizabeth, his wife, widow of the late John Shelton, lord of the manor of West Bromwich, granted a 21-year lease to Philip Foley, of, among other things, 'the forge hammer mill, consisting of two fineries and a chafere' called West Bromwich Forge.[13]

About this time the Whorwood family obtained some control over the activity at the forge even though not possession of the mill itself. Philip Foley obtained from Brome Whorwood of Sandwell a lease for 21 years from 1673 of the 'watercourse of Tame used with a cornmill called Joane Mill in West Bromwich and used to a forge hammer mill called West Bromwich Forge.'[14] The lease at that time probably only applied to the part of the Tame which ran through Monk's Meadow which belonged to the

Whorwoods. In 1684, Elizabeth Whorwood of London, 'Relict of William Whorwood Esq.' (of Sandwell) obtained a lease for 98 years from William Turton, ironmonger, of West Bromwich, for 2s. 6d. and an annual peppercorn rent, of 'all those Watercourses runninge fromwards Joane Bridge downe towards Bromwich fforge'.[15] This suggests that from that time the Whorwoods had control of both river and leat from their Monk's Meadow upstream to the weir at Joan Bridge. It is not clear from an examination of the Turton genealogy which William this is, though it is probable that he was a member of the 'Oak House' rather than of the 'Mill' branch.

The annual inventory for the forges in 1672, as in other years, shows entries for both 'charcoles' and 'seacoles', the former always in much larger quantities than the latter. It would be interesting to know in which part of the process each was used.

One item from the stock account of March 1673 is, '2 pr. great Wheeles at Bromwich, £10'. We surmise that these were waterwheels, probably made on the site and stored to be used in the locality.

By 1676, Foley had decided to reduce his immediate interest in the operation of the Stour valley complex. An agreement was signed, 28 February 1676, whereby, in consideration of the sum of £500, Philip Foley of Prestwood was to transfer to Humphrey Jennens of Earlington (Erdington?), Warwickshire, the working of the Bromwich, Wednesbury and Little Aston Forges and the Bustleholme Mill and associated watercourses for the duration of the outstanding period of their respective lease.[16] That Foley retained an interest in the working is shown by the 1678 entries in his accounts for repairs to the various buildings and that in 1679 he drew up another agreement with Jennens defining the limits of the activities of the latter in the matter of source of raw materials and the sale of produce in order not to harm the interests of other groups within the complex.[17] It should be noted that Jennens does not appear in the local manorial records, but that Philip Foley is listed as defaulter in each of the years 1685-6-7.

Jennens's interest ceased with the expiration of the lease, which was renewed in October 1691, by John Shelton, lord of the manor of West Bromwich to Philip Foley for one year for the sum of £20. The forge was stated to be in the tenure of Philip Foley.[18] It will be noted that the lease of the watercourse was of a later date than that of the forge, and this explains the memorandum that 'Mr. Jennens has three years in Mr. Whorwood's watercourse. Mr. Foley to agree to have it at the same rent of Mr. Jennens else Bromwich Forge cannot work'.[19] This was dated 1691. The 1695 West Bromwich manorial rent roll states that Foley had renewed the lease in 1692 for a further period of 20 years.[20] He was then paying a collective rent of £60 per year for the 'Rodmill and fforge'.

By the beginning of the next century new names had appeared. In 1714, John and Thomas Adams of the forge were held to be in default for having failed to present themselves at the local court leat[21] while in the same year, John Shelton, the last of that name to hold the lordship of the manor, granted a 21-year lease of the forge[22] to Richard Geast of Handsworth who was already in possession of the building. It further states that John Adams and Joseph Colman were the occupants of the two cottages. This lease provides interesting information on the state of the forge, which then consisted of a 'forge hamer water-mill or Ironwork, two ffinerys and one Charfy'. As an allowance for maintenance and repairs, it granted to Richard Geast, 'liberty to get, dig, take or use, stones, turfs, land or clay from the Comon of the said Manor of West Bromwich for the doing and making of bricks' and 'liberty to fetch pitcoles gratis at the colepits of the said John Shelton'. However this was limited to the 'burning of four clamps of bricks'. Provision was also made for timber for the maintenance of the wheel and the main hammer-beam. Regulations were provided as to the use of underwood, brush and coppice timber to be used for charcoal-making. Despite the pleas of Dud Dudley over half a century earlier, it seems that charcoal was still used on the forge hearths. The coal-pits referred to were probably in Wednesbury.

The work at the forge at this time was insufficient to provide a full-time occupation and both cottagers were venturing into small-scale agriculture. In 1719 both Adams and Coleman were paying rent for small areas of ground.[23] From the 1720 *Terrier* we gather that the Adams family were renting 13½ acres, known as Biddles Crofts, but no farm buildings, so presumably they were being worked from the forge cottage.[24] Another interesting fact to emerge from the same document, was that the forge pool, of which Mr. Richard Geast was the lessee, covered some 14½ acres, a large area for so small an undertaking. This is of course strictly in line with what we know of the topography and the shallow nature of the pool.

The Geast lease could not have run its full period, for a Mr. Thomas Powell, ironmaster, of Dudley in the county of Worcester, was granted a 12-year lease from Lady Day 1725.[25] In the same year Thomas Powell obtained from the Earl of Dartmouth, who had acquired the Whorwood estates, a 21-year lease, at a rent of £21 per annum, of the same watercourses mentioned above.[26] This lease contains reference to the 'ffurnace now decayed'.

Thomas Powell's stay must have been very short for he was succeeded by Mr. Edward Kendall, who left behind him more of a record.[27] For example, he purchased some eight and a half tons of pig-iron between 1727 and 1732 from the Hales Furnace and 73 tons of rod or bar from the Stour valley subsidiary forges in the same period.[28] This suggests that he was probably obtaining pig iron from other sources and that, at the same time, he was also running a business as an 'ironmonger' selling rod to the nailing community. Of course, it is possible that the Stour Forge purchases were all bar iron, since no distinction is made in the accounts between bar and rod, and that this bar was being reduced to rod at the West Bromwich Old Forge.

In 1742, the forge was leased for a period of 21 years to John Churchill, ironmaster of Hints Forge in the County of Stafford, another name in the growth of the Midland iron industry.[29] This lease ran its full term. It is interesting to note that in his *View of Staffordshire* (1735) Dr. Wilkes states that there was but one forge in West Bromwich at that time. It was during the Churchill era that from 1758 to 1764, Francis Asbury, later to become a leading figure in the Methodist Church, was reputed to have been apprenticed to a certain Mr. Foxall, foreman of the Old Forge.[30] It has not been possible to confirm this statement.

In 1762, Churchill obtained from the Earl of Dartmouth a lease of the watercourse for a period 21 years on terms similar to the Powell lease,[31] and in the following year he renewed the lease of the mill for the period of a further 21 years at the previous rent.[32] This was doomed to an early termination for in less than four years it had passed into the hands of Wright and Jesson, local West Bromwich families.

Here we might pause for a moment to look at the part the Jessons were playing in the local iron trade. It was an old family mentioned in local records as far back as the 15th century. In the early part of the 18th century Thomas Jesson was adding to the family fortunes as an 'ironmonger'.[33] His first three sons predeceased him and it fell to the lot of the fourth son, Joseph, to carry on the family traditions, which he effectively did, taking up the business about 1750. From time to time over the next 10 years he was buying rod from the Stour valley forges.[34] In 1762, he took into partnership his younger brother, Richard, then aged 21, and they continued together until 1766-7, by which time Richard was living at Cooper's Hill in West Bromwich. Prior to this, Ann Jesson, their sister, had married John Wright of the Manwoods, on the Handsworth boundary. He came of another family of ironmongers then working in this locality, and he combined the tasks of nailmaster, farmer,

and steward of the Earl of Dartmouth's estates at
Sandwell. In 1766-7 John Wright and Richard Jesson
combined forces, taking over the forge and purchasing
their first consignment of pig iron from the Aston
Furnaces.[35] We are told that the firm obtained letters
patent in 1774 for the making of malleable iron from pig
iron using coal and no fluxes.[36] However, we cannot
imagine that they made a fortune, for in 1776 they
borrowed £200 from brother Joseph to maintain their
business and three years later another £500 to promote
their trade in Shropshire.[37] They continued to pay
interest on these loans until 1801. When John Wright
died, about the middle of the 1770s, Richard Jesson
continued with his nephew, Richard Wright, who took
over his father's interests. Thus, for a time, the firm
became Jesson and Wright.

In 1785, the forge received an interesting and important
visitor, Matthew Boulton. He provides us with valuable
information.[38] The forge was no longer a hammer-mill
but a rolling and slitting-mill. We have no indication
of the date of conversion to a slitting-mill, but it was
certainly after 1714 and not by the Foleys, a surprising
fact since they introduced this process to the area. It
was still a small undertaking for, from these notes, we
learn that there were only four men employed, one being
the foreman, whose responsibility it was to keep the
rolls and slitters in order. The process was not continuous,
nor could the capacity of three tons per day be increased,
owing to the lack of water power. The installation of a
steam-engine would be necessary to increase output.
This never happened. Interesting customs of the trade
emerge. The ironmaster supplied the master roller at the
rate of 21cwt. per 'ton', receiving back rods at 20cwt.
per ton, 120lb. being allowed to the cwt. in each case.
The extra hundredweight was not clear profit to the mill
for Boulton estimated that each yielded a half hundredweight of cut rods, a quarter hundredweight of scrap rod
and a quarter hundredweight of 'waste' for which there
was a sale, at a price.

On a later visit in 1792, Matthew Boulton stated that there were two wheels, each of 10ft. diameter and with ladles 4ft. 6in. wide.[39] There was a head of water of four to four and a half feet, which means that they were breast or possibly undershot wheels. He adds that Mr. Wright informed him that there was a total fall and head of about 22ft. 6in. This would involve a lade of over a mile in length; that is in line with what we have known in recent times.

The firm continued for some little time yet, though the growth of large-scale industry, which was now appearing in other parts of the parish, passed this site by. Stebbing Shaw, writing in 1798, recorded that Messrs. Jesson and Wright were operating the slitting-mill there.[40] Richard Jesson, at least, had prospered, for he was now living at 'The Leveretts', a large house just over the Handsworth boundary. He became High Sheriff of Staffordshire in 1804, at the age of 63. When he died, prior to 1817, he was survived by a son, Thomas, and a daughter, Elizabeth, who was married to Samuel Dawes, member of another 'iron family'. On the death of his father-in-law, Samuel Dawes and his wife went to live at 'The Leveretts', and he it was who entered the firm, changing the name of the business, by that time moved to Bromford Lane, to Jesson and Dawes, and later to S. and J. Dawes, Bromford Iron and Steel Co.[41] The firm actually took over the Bromford Mill at the turn of the century, when it was known as the ironworks of Wright and Jesson,[42] but it is uncertain whether this represents the removal of the firm from the Old Forge or a period of expansion when they were working the two mills simultaneously.

Reeves tells us that with the end of the reign of Jesson and Wright, the forge was operated by James Halford, but if so he left little to record.[43]

By 1818 we find that the forge was being worked by Charles Bache, ironmaster.[44] Reeves adds the information that Bache worked the slitting-mill, obtaining his bar iron from J. Bagnall and Sons, Golds Green.

The end of the manorial estates of West Bromwich was approaching, and in 1823 they were under the hammer. Part of Lot 31 consisted of the forge, buildings, Forge Pool, yards, osier beds, etc., occupying just under 16 acres and leased to Charles Bache for six years as from Lady Day 1823. The purchaser was the Earl of Dartmouth, and Bache did not stay, for in the same year he moved his works to Great Bridge.[45] This was the end of the iron era for West Bromwich Old Forge. Reeves, writing in 1836 brings the picture up to date: 'a smelting furnace formerly stood in a meadow to the South-West of the pool. The forge has been in ruins several years and the mill, used for slitting iron, about a quarter of a mile distant, is now a corn mill'.[46]

It is not at all clear whether the corn mill of Reeves's time was worked on a commercial scale for it is not until 1845 that we find it advertised as 'William Harris of the Slitting Flour Mill, near Manwoods'.[47] Five years later it is called the 'Old Forge Mill' with 'Harris & Smith' as the millers.[48] Harris must have started early in business as he was only 29 at the time of the 1851 census. The continuity of flour-mills over these dates, as shown by directories, is a little curious as the Tithe Schedule of 1849 shows the Earl of Dartmouth as owner and the mill as a 'saw-mill', both the mill and mill-pool being in hand at that date. Perhaps the Tithe Schedule was an error, the saw-mill being the adjacent 'Sandwell Mill'.

From 1858 to 1865, various directories show that it was being worked by the Thompson family, a directory of the last date showing 'George Thompson, Miller and Malster'. From that date to 1884 it is omitted from directories, suggesting that competition from the numerous steam-driven mills in the district was too great. The gap may be partly filled, however, as Thomas Beeson, from the neighbouring Wigmore Farm and Joan Mill, joined his son John at the Forge Mill in 1873, to run the combined farm and corn mill. They had little chance to prove their success for a 'distress warrant' was issued against them and the sale was held in January 1874.

The pair of millstones raised £1 7s.[49] Pheonix-like, the mill was to rise again, if only for a short time, for the 1884 *Kelly's Directory* shows that Richard Smith was listed as the (water) miller at the Forge Mill. Smith was succeeded by Miles Summerton who was working there as a corn miller until at least 1890.

From that time it lapsed to the status of a 'grist mill', grinding grain for animal fodder for neighbouring farmers, a task which it continued to perform until the First World War, as I was informed in 1950 by Mr. Skidmore, the then occupant. He added the interesting information that it took three days to fill the pool and only eight hours to empty it, an indication of the degree of silting which had taken place since Boulton's visit. About 1914 the pool was emptied for the last time and converted into a somewhat damp pasture and the mill finally dismantled. In 1969 the position of the wheel and sluices could still be seen, while the mill-stones formed part of the flooring of the yard.

NOTES

1.   Jos. Reeves, *History of West Bromwich* (1836), p. 112.

2.   John Izon, 'A Handsworth Case in the Court of Star Chamber', *Birmingham Post* (19 June 1952).

3.   *Staffordshire Quarter Session Rolls* (1597), (*S.H.C.*, 1932, pp. 298-300).

4.   *Staffordshire Quarter Session Rolls* (1602), (*S.H.C.*, 1935, p. 438).

5.   West Bromwich Manorial Court Roll, 1606.

6.   *Ibid.*, 1609.

7.   *Ibid.*, 1619.

8.   West Bromwich Manorial Rent Roll, 1626.

9.   *Ibid.*, 1630.

10.   *Ibid.*, 1649

11.   *Staffordshire Hearth Tax Roll* (1666), (*S.H.C.*, 1925, pp. 246-52).

12.   Hereford County Record Office, F/VI/KBF/2-22.

13.   *Ibid.*, F/VI/KG/3 *et seq.*

14.   *Ibid.*, F/VI/KG/3 *et seq,*

15.   Stafford County Record Office, D 564/3/1/23.

16.   Hereford County Record Office, F/VI/KG/1 *et seq.*

17.   *Ibid.*, F/VI/KG/8.

18. *Ibid.*, F/VI/KG/7.
19. *Ibid.*, F/VI/KG/1.
20. West Bromwich Manorial Rent Roll, 1695.
21. West Bromwich Manorial Court Roll, 1714.
22. Birmingham Reference Library, 378063.
23. West Bromwich Manorial Rent Roll, 1719.
24. West Bromwich Manorial *Terrier*, 1720.
25. West Bromwich Manorial Rent Roll, 1731.
26. Stafford County Record Office, D 564/3/2/6.
27. An amendment on West Bromwich Manorial Rent Roll, 1731.
28. Knight's Account Books; Kidderminster Reference Library.
29. An amendment on West Bromwich Manorial Rent Roll, 1731.
30. James Lewis, *Francis Asbury, Bishop of the Methodist Episcopalian Church* (1927), pp. 16-17.
31. Stafford County Record Office, D 564/3/2/6.
32. West Bromwich Manorial Rent Roll, 1761.
33. Collection of Jesson Deeds; West Bromwich Reference Library.
34. Knight's Account Books.
35. *Ibid.*
36. Jos. Reeves, *op. cit.*, p. 112.
37. Account Book, Jesson Deeds No. 119.
38. Matthew Boulton, *MS. Note Book*, Birmingham Assay Office.
39. *Ibid.*
40. Stebbing Shaw, *op. cit.*, p. 117.
41. *Parson and Bradshaw Directory* (1818).
42. West Bromwich Enclosure Award Map, 1801-4.
43. Jos. Reeves, *op. cit.*, p. 112.
44. *Parson and Bradshaw Directory* (1818).
45. *Ward and Price Directory* (1823).
46. Jos. Reeves, *op. cit.*, p. 112.
47. *Post Office Directory* (1845).
48. *Slater's Classified Directory* (1850).
49. Stafford County Record Office, D 564/8/1/14.

VIII

JONE (JOANNE or JOAN) MILL

One of the least significant and consequently least documented of the mills was Jone Mill (023936) in Wigmore Lane, West Bromwich, close to the present motorway crossing of that lane. The name itself is something of a puzzle, for we have no knowledge of its origin. An early reference to the name Joan is contained in a Deed of 1577 which mentions a lane from Hately Heath to Joanne Bridge.[1] This was a bridge over the Tame, where the road from West Bromwich Manor to Great Barr, now known as Charlemont Road (021939), crossed it. This bridge was still so named on the Enclosure map of 1804. The mill is shrouded in mystery. Who, or what, was Joan? Why was the bridge named Joan Bridge? Was it built by some long-forgotten medieval benefactress? Was the mill, half a mile downstream named independently or after the bridge? Was the mill always on the same site? When was it first built? Was any attempt made to convert it to iron work? These and many other questions may never be answered satisfactorily.

The earliest reference to the mill itself that we can find is contained in the survey of the property of the Sandwell Priory at the time of the Dissolution in 1526. '[Anne Heles] holdeth by indenture a water miln for corne . . . on the water of Tame called Jone Miln wt ij medowez bel' to the . . . wt a little Croft like a garden which medowez ben send wt the seid water & cont' iiij acr' & butts on the estside on Barr Medow & on the northend on Jone Bridge & on the s. . . . and westside on a lane ledyng from Gryndersford toward Waddyer . . . & Paieth yerelie for the same 23s. 4d. . . . Item, the seid milln is in dekay for lack of Tymber'.[2]

According to John Izon (*see* the previous chapter)
Thomas Parkes of Wednesbury was granted permission,
in 1585, by Walter Stanley, lord of the manor of
West Bromwich, to dig a mill lade from a bridge at
Grinder's Ford to the lane from Haie Pits to Handsworth,
the present Forge Lane. This raises the question of
Grinder's Ford'. The suggestion is of a bridge close to
an old ford near to a blade-mill. Old maps and records
reveal but three ancient bridges over this part of the
river: the 'Tame' bridge on the West Bromwich to Walsall
road; Jone Bridge on the old road from West Bromwich
Manor to Barr; and that on the present Newton Road.
This last may be ruled out by the agreed termination
of the lade. The first is improbable because the lade
would then have to run past Bustleholme, which we
believe to have been already in existence. That leaves
Jone Bridge, but if so why not use the name by which it
was already known? The nearest mill to that bridge would
be Bustleholme. Does that mean that Bustleholme was a
'grinder's mill' or blade-mill in 1585? Or was there
another mill of which we know nothing?

The lade, a mile long, was excavated from the weir
just above Jone Bridge down to the Old Forge and soon
afterwards we find 'Jone Mill' about half-way along the
route. This raises interesting speculations. Was it actually
drawing water at that time from the same mill lade?
This would be to the detriment of a lower mill. Would the
lord of the manor or his lessee permit such encroachment
by a third party? Yet a third party there must have been
for this mill at no time figures in the Manorial Rent Rolls.
Is it not more probable that it was not on the exact site
and that it had a separate supply of water? That it was
close to the lane is confirmed by the statement made
in 1602 by 'John Partridge of Smethwicke' that he was
in the lane by Jane Mill, at that time flooded by the
overflowing of the lade.[3] The alternative would have to be
a pool, but where? If it was on the left bank of the river,
the mill would have been in Barr Parish, not West
Bromwich. In this case the river would have separated

Plate 1: The Sandwell mill-pool, 1907. (Photo: H. Thompson)

Plate 2: West Bromwich Old Forge, *c.* 1880. (Painting: F. Willis Price)

Plate 3: Bustleholme Mill, 1968. (Photo: A. Price)

Plate 4: Joan Mill, 1925. (Photo: E. Lissimore)

Plate 5: West Bromwich Old Forge Mill, 1906. (Photo: G. Allen)

Plate 6: Hamstead Mill, *c.* 1897. (Photo: Anon)

Plate 7: Wednesbury Forge, late 19th century.

the mill from the lane and later documents quote its position as being in West Bromwich. Half a mile or so to the south-west of this site is a spring, which gave rise to a small brooklet, flowing to the Tame nearby, a stream too insignificant to be marked on the 1in. O.S. map. Was a small dam thrown up across this brooklet? If this were so, the original mill may well have been within a few yards of its last known position. Unfortunately the construction of the motorway in 1968 so changed the topography here that inspection of the ground is now impossible. The brook is now contained in a drain.

In 1606 Richard Parkes, operating the West Bromwich Old Forge, 'raised or stopped up the watercourse at Johan Mill pool tayle, so that Thomas Walstead and his tenants are hindered in their entry, egress and regress with their beasts to the meadow'.[4] Here we have clear evidence of a mill pool on the West Bromwich side of the Tame. The 'tail', the water flowing from the mill, must have flowed into the lade which was on the same side of the river. The later position of the mill was between the lade and the river, where there was no room for a dam. If we accept that the mill was supplied by this anonymous brooklet, we can see that its usefulness would be extremely limited and that at no time would it attract the interest of the iron industry.

For the next hundred years we find no references to the mill, though several to the bridge and the adjacent meadows. In 1673 Brome Whorwood of Sandwell leased for 21 years to Philip Foley, 'the watercourses of the Tame used with a cornmill called Jane Mill in West Bromwich and used to a forge hammer mill called West Bromwich Forge'.[5] This tells us not only the use of the mill and that by this time the mill appeared to be using the common lade, but that part of the lade at least was running through ground held by the Whorwoods of Sandwell and not the lord of the manor. The explanation of this is probably to be found in the sale of parts of the Wigmore Common Field during the preceding century.[6] The land and site were the property of the Dartmouths, successors of the Whorwoods, at Sandwell, in the early part of this century.

The Whorwoods obtained a firmer hold on the watercourse when Elizabeth Whorwood, widow, obtained in 1684, a 98-year lease from William Turton of 'all those watercourses Runninge fromwards Joane Bridge downe towards Bromwich Forge through a meadowe late of Brome Whorwood, deceased'.[7]

In 1725 and again in 1762 the Earl of Dartmouth leased the watercourses to the lessees, Thomas Powell and John Churchill respectively, of the Old Forge Mill.[8] Both leases, using almost identical wording, refer to the 'Water and Watercourse of the River Tame, heretofore belonging and used to and with a Certain Corne Mill called Joan Mill situated and being in West Bromwich'. The wording, though somewhat ambiguous, suggests that the mill was no longer extant and that it worked from the lade. It is explicit, however, that 'the watercourse extendeth from the Upper end of the Green or Waste above Joan Bridge'. The foundation of the weir at that point is still to be seen.

It is possible that the mill had temporarily vanished. Reeves, writing in 1832, describing the course of the Tame, lists some of the mills passed, omits Joan Mill, but refers to Wigmore, a general term for the area.[9] The 1851 census return has no mention of the mill but gives the address of Thomas Beeson, living and farming there, as 6 Wigmore. John Keeming had occupied the farm 17 years before,[10] but was succeeded by Beeson in 1845, he remaining there until 1873. After a period in the hands of John Haden, farm bailiff of the Earl of Dartmouth, it was occupied by James Smith. Willetts said in 1882, 'near Wigmore, close to the road leading to Great Barr (Newton Road) stands a farm, now in the occupation of Mr. James Smith, which we believe to be "Jone Mill". There is at present a water wheel, put in by the late Mr. Beeson, but the diversion we speak of was made long before this time'.[11]

Purely as a farm grist mill it survived throughout the rest of the century. The derelict mill and house were demolished in 1955 by Mr. Thompson the tenant at that time.

NOTES

1. M. Willett, *op. cit.*, p. 216.
2. P.R.O., E 36/165, f. 132.
3. *Staffordshire Quarter Session Rolls* (1602), (*S.H.C.*, 1935, p. 437).
4. West Bromwich Manorial Court Roll, 1606.
5. A. J. Bartley, *Social and Economic Development of Wednesbury, 1650-1750* (1967), M.A. Thesis of London University.
6. M. Willett, *op. cit.*, pp. 206-220.
7. Stafford County Record Office, D 564/3/1/23.
8. Stafford County Record Office, D 564/3/2/6.
9. Jos. Reeves, *op. cit.*, pp. 5-6.
10. *White's Staffordshire Directory* (1834).
11. M. Willett, *op. cit.*, p. 192.

IX

BUSTLEHOLME MILL

That Bustleholme is the site of one of the earliest mills in this area is an indisputable fact. A mill here was quite probably one of those referred to in the Final Concord of 1567 when Thomas Comberford, lord of the Manor of Wednesbury, purchased four water grain mills.[1] It may have originated as a corn mill, or the blade-mill of 1585 (*see* chapter XIII), but none of these possibilites can we be certain. As previously stated, most early documents fail to give the name or the exact location when dealing with houses or mills. This was possibly the 'Grinder's' Mill of 1526, mentioned in chapter VIII. The earliest specific documentation of the Bustleholme Mill is the Final Concord conveying the property from Thomas Comberford, of the Manor of Wednesbury, to Walter Stanley, lord of the manor of West Bromwich, and dated 20 February 1594.[2] This sale included the mill, together with 'all right, claim and demand in all those floodgates upon the water of the Tame near Bustleholme in West Bromwich, and of the soil whereon the floodgates stand, and all that parcel of ground, stank or dam, in length 30 yards and in breadth 15 yards'. It will be seen that little enough is said in the way of description and yet that little, together with what is not said, may enable us to draw some mental picture of the edifice. Despite the steeper gradient and consequent faster current of the Tame, it was found necessary to construct a lade. Even this was insufficient to provide the required head of water, so a dam was constructed. Now dam is an ambiguous word. It may mean the earthen bank or the area of water retained behind it. In this document, the use of the alternative 'stank' suggests that the latter use is intended.

In this case, the dimensions quoted give an amazingly small dam; an area approximately the same as that of a house building plot of the 1930s. This would store but little water, and so we come to the conclusion that it was an insignificant establishment by comparison with others, even in this area. And what of its use? There is no mention of this but if it were a blade-mill or was otherwise connected with the iron trade such would probably have been stated. It was far away from the common open fields and nucleated settlements. Hence our conclusion that at the end of the 16th century, Bustleholme was a very small corn mill, doing little business, combined with a blade-mill.

This was the period at which the water power of the Tame was being harnessed for the benefit of the infant iron industry, and the water mill was supplanting the manual forge. It is probable that Walter Stanley bought Bustleholme with this in view but we know nothing of its history for the next 30 years.

It was from Lady Day 1625 that a lease of 'two water-mills under one roof' for 10 years was granted to Hugh Woodman and John Reignolds, for £20 a year.[3] We are told that the tenants of the said mills are to leave them in as good 'repayre at ye end of their terme as they are now in within very sufficient'. We still know nothing of the mill, but it seems probable that Woodman was the ironmaster financing the operations with the assistance of John Reynolds, who was a local man, and who later rented a cottage and smallholding of 28½ acres of land near to this mill.

This lease was to have an early termination, for three years later, in 1628, Sir Edward Peytoe and Mr. Roger Fowke, became the lessees for a period of 21 years at an annual rent of £21.[4] It is almost certain that the mill had become part of the iron industry by this time as both of these gentlemen are known to have been so involved in other places. An interesting side note on the 1630 Rent Roll, referring to a possible future increase in rent, 'q(uery) how their Ingine will prove', suggests that new machinery had recently been installed. What sort of machinery? Hackwood states that Bustleholme was a blade-mill at the time of the Civil War, that is, towards the end of this lease.[5]

The next tenants of the mill were Messrs. Thomas Foley, of 'Stirdbridge' in Worcestershire, and Gerard Fowke, of Tunson in the County of Stafford, according to an indenture between these two and John Shelton, the then lord of the manor of West Bromwich, and dated 7 May 1650.[6] It granted the lease for 21 years and stated that the 'Bustleholme Millnes' consisted of 'one Corne Millne' and a slitting-mill.

It may be relevant at this point to consider the people connected with the mill at this time. Firstly there was the owner, the lord of the manor. Then there were the lessees, Messrs. Foley and Fowke, paying the rent to the owner and directing the operation of the mill as one of the numerous small mills which formed the Foley 'empire'. Next there were the people resident on the spot: the foreman manager or miller, who lived in the larger mill-house and occupied the farm which was always part of this establishment, and the two or three workmen, usually occupying the two cottages on the site. At the time of the 1650 lease, William Ford was the resident manager, but the only occupant of the cottages was a Widow Tibbetts.

A note on the 17th-century residents at the Bustleholme Mill, which must not be confused with 'Bustleholme', the adjacent farm to the south-west, residence of the Symcox family, throws some light on the status of such people. The Ford family had been in West Bromwich for over a hundred years, apparently as husbandmen. They accumulated sufficient wealth to join the class of yeoman farmers. In 1637, and again in 1639, Henry Ford was purchasing land in the parish. At that time he is described 'mylner', though at what mill we are not informed. It was probably at Bustleholme under Messrs. Peytoe and Fowke. Before he died in 1666, his son william had taken over at Bustleholme as is evidenced by the above 1650 lease. William was a man of substance, for in addition to his activity as miller, he was farming adjacent land on his own account and paying rent to the manor,[7] and purchasing land from time to time. In the assessment for the hearth tax in 1666 he was assessed for four hearths. This indicates that he occupied one of the larger houses in the West Bromwich of that time and it appears that the old mill house at Bustleholme, now in ruins, probably dates from the occupancy of the Fords. On the death of William in 1672, it is revealed that the family possessed estate in Smethwick and Handsworth as well as West Bromwich. The winding up of the family affairs was conducted by one Henry Ford, brother of William, and a lawyer of Lincoln's Inn Fields in London.

Another man connected with the mill at this time was that of the Avery (variously Avory, Avrill, Averill and Averell) family. They had been resident in the district for some time before they moved to the mill, presumably into the workman's cottages, shortly after 1650. The parish register records the marriage of Henry Avrill and Mary Wyley in 1641, and the christening of their several children over the next few years, but it is not until 1656 that they are referred to as being of the Rodmill. In the same year we find the marriage of Raphael Avory, presumably brother of Henry, servant of Mr. Thomas Foley, to Margaret Elton, daughter of a Walsall weaver. A year later, 1657, is the entry of the christening of William, son of Raphael and Margaret Avory of the Rodmill. Their sojourn at the mill must have been short, for at the time of the 1666 hearth tax, William Ford was at the Mill House, as mentioned above, and in the two cottages 'Widdow Avery and Widdow Tibbats', the latter having lived there for at least 16 years. On the death of William Ford, Richard Wheeler became manager of the mill.

After Thomas Foley shared out his empire in 1667, a new lease was prepared on 14 September 1669, whereby Walter Needham and his wife Elizabeth, widow of the late John Shelton, leased to Philip Foley for 21 years the Bustleholme corn mill and slitting-mill.[8] In

1676 Philip Foley agreed to sub-let the mill together
with the forges at Little Aston, Wednesbury, and West
Bromwich (*q.v.*) to Humphrey Jennens for the duration
of the unexpired portion of the lease. In 1691 a lease
was prepared from John Shelton to Philip Foley of 'that
messuage, barns and stables, corn mill and slitting mill
called Bustleholme Mill' as from Lady Day 1692 for one
year at a rent of £40,[9] later renewed for 20 years. During
this period it was sub-leased to John Jennens.

Philip Foley is listed as a defaulter for non-attendance
at the manorial court in 1686 and again in 1689,[10] an
occurrence all too likely for a non-resident lessee of
property within the manor. Thomas Foley had died
in 1677.

In 1679, Richard Harrison was resident at the Rodmill,
while James Smith, junior, was a 'Carrier of Busslome
ware' in 1707.[11]

The 1692 lease did not run its full term. At this time
the manor was once more in financial difficulties and
properties were being sold. In 1709, John Shelton, the
last of that name to hold the lordship of the manor,
sold Bustleholme to John Lowe, an ironmonger of Lyndon
in West Bromwich.[12] He was a dealer in iron, principally
as nail rod to the nailers of the district. The mill was
described as 'one corn mill and one slitting mill joined
together', thus retaining the dual nature that it probably
always possessed. The fact that the conveyance included
a 'cinder bank', 10yds. wide and 49yds. long, leads to
speculation as to its nature and value. Was this 'cinder
bank' a store of coked coal purchased for use on the
hearth? It seems a rather large amount for the require-
ments of so small an establishment. Or was it an
accumulation of iron-rich clinker from a forge? In that
case it is surprising that it had not been sold to a furnace
for reclamation.

In 1732 John Lowe transferred the mill to his son,
Jesson Lowe.[13] Again it had a dual capacity, but this
time as a rod-mill and as an oil mill. The latter is an
unusual use in this part of the world, but is scarcely

surprising when one considers the number of references to the growing of flax, hemp and rape in the district. Bilston in particular appears to have been quite an important centre of flax growing.[14]

Though neither of the above conveyances refers to a forge or hammer-mill, it seems probable that one did exist incorporated with the rod-mill. In 1727, Jesson Lowe, no doubt working with his father at that time, was the purchaser of pig iron from the Hales Furnace[15] and again he appears in similar transactions at both the Hales and Aston furnaces from 1751 until his death in 1758. This suggests that at that time he was making some of his own bar for the slitting-mill. On the other hand he did not purchase any bar from the Stour valley forges after 1745 when he was paying £3 3s. per ton for the transport of the bar from Wolverly to West Bromwich. The amounts he was buying were small and quite inadequate even for Bustleholme, and we must conclude that he was purchasing from other sources as well. We have additional evidence that forge work was being undertaken here from an advertisement for a farm, situated between Mr. Jesson Lowe's house (Charlemont Hall) and Tame Bridge and adjacent to a 'forge and slitting Mill'.[16]

When Jesson Lowe took over the mill in 1732, the tenant was Moses Harper, who later branched out as an ironmonger in his own right, purchasing rod from Stour valley up to 1770.

From the death of Jesson Lowe until the end of the century the history of the mill is something of a mystery, though Reeves states that a Mr. Leonard was working the slitting-mill about 1770.[17] This fact has yet to be confirmed but it may well be, for in 1801 a Mr. Charles Leonard was in possession of land next to the mill site.[18] This Mr. Leonard died before 1804.[19]

The next definite knowledge that we have of the mill is that it was occupied by W. Chapman, farmer and bayonet-maker.[20] Thus the days of the slitting-mill were over and by now it had become a blade-mill. This is in

line with the other Midland mills which survived until
the middle of this century in some cases, but only as
water-powered scythe- or blade-mills.

During the first two decades of the 19th century James
Smith of Hall Green House, West Bromwich, was making
extensive purchases of property in the district. At what
date he acquired the mill is uncertain, but in 1819 he
leased Bustleholme Mill for 21 years to Thomas and
William Morris, ironmasters of Bradley, William Chapman
still being tenant at the time.[21] The property included
the mill, two workmen's cottages, warehouses, buildings,
barns, stabling, etc. Some 69 acres of land provided for
the agriculture which was still part of the activity at the
mill. The lease gives an interesting and detailed account
of the mill equipment. The waterwheel consisted of three
cast-iron rings with wrought-iron ladles. The shaft, fly-
wheel and gears, in fact most of the machinery, was
of cast iron with brass bearings. There was also a brick
support for the roll-bed-framing. As all this apparatus
was new it is obvious that the mill was being converted
from a blade-mill to a rolling-mill. In fact in 1823
Thomas Morris is described as an iron-roller.[22] Nevertheless, the days of Bustleholme, as part of the iron industry,
were coming to an end, as they were in the case of most
other small water mills.

In 1829, James Smith died without issue, and his estate
passed to the hands of his nephews, named Dorsett, to
be held in trust for a number of legatees, members of
the family. The Smith Trustees, or Dorsett Trustees as
they came to be known, administered the Trust for
almost a hundred years.

In the next year the Morris lease was not renewed and
George Dorsett, one of Smith's nephews, took over the
mill, converting it to a corn mill only. He operated
the mill himself and appears in the 1835 Directory
as 'miller'.[23] When Reeves wrote his *History of West
Bromwich* in 1836, he names the same George Dorsett
as the miller.

In 1839 the trustees of James Smith granted a seven-year lease to Messrs. Baker and Evans, the latter being described as the miller and the former as a malster. The mill had been previously advertised in Aris's *Birmingham Gazette,* and the *Birmingham Herald* as a water corn mill working three pairs of 'french stones'. With the mill went the farm, two cottages and about 100 acres of land. Dorsett himself had been living at the Mill House, while John Harris occupied one of the cottages. There is a full account of the mill equipment and a description of the large house in the schedule of the lease.

The construction of the Tame Valley Canal in about 1840, which passes so close to the buildings on the top of its aqueduct, might well have brought operations to an end for it cut right across the mill end of the dam. As it was, a culvert was provided beneath the embankment and the mill continued to use the dam, now reduced in size, to the north of the canal. One can imagine the difficulty created for the miller who was now cut off from easy access to the sluices and control gates.

The next lease, dated 1846, was to John Woodward, miller, for a period of 14 years and included the same buildings and about 72 acres of land.[25] This lease contains a number of restrictions and limitations on the agriculture but gives no details of the mill. John Woodward appears as a miller in a number of documents. A most interesting fact is that by 1855 he had moved his residence to Hollyhedge Road, a newly-developing road in West Bromwich, while still working the mill.[26]

In 1851 the census return shows that the residents on the site were John Woodward, farmer and miller, and Thomas Bailey, the miller's waggoner. In addition the miller employed two labourers living elsewhere.

In 1860 the water corn mill, farm, two cottages (one empty), buildings and land were leased to George Ryland, miller, for 14 years.[27] It is described as being lately in the occupation of John Woodward and his sub-tenants. The lease contains the stipulation that should a steam-engine be installed at the mill, it was to become the property of the trustees at the expiration of the lease. A new waterwheel had just been provided, a huge one for so small a mill. It was 17ft. in diameter and 7ft. wide, made with cast-iron rings, fitted with curved wrought-iron ladles a quarter of an inch thick. The whole was mounted on a hollow cylindrical shaft.

It seems probable that George Ryland sub-let the mill, for from this time on the local directories provide us with the names of a series of tenants, all of them combining the occupations of farmer and miller. In 1860 there was Robert Thomas, Thomas Thomas in 1868, Wyburn Leadbeater in 1872, Charles Leadbeater in 1873 (electoral register), and Gaspar Hewkins (Hukins) in 1880 and 1884.

By 1897, as may be imagined, there had been so many changes among the interested beneficiaries and trustees of the Smith-Dorsett trust, that it was necessary to clarify and legalise the situation by an involved and lengthy deed.[28] This names the tenants at that time as William and Walter Simcox and William Hickinbottom. In 1904, the mill was in the same hands. When Hackwood was writing in 1908 he satisfied himself by saying that the mill was still working, but he gave no details.[29] We do know, however, that after Messrs. Simcox and Hickinbottom parted company, William Hickinbottom continued as tenant, to be succeeded in turn by John Saunders.

Mr. Lester, the tenant in 1970, informs me that in the first decade of this century the mill was worked in turn by a Mr. Dale, a Mr. Green, and was leased by E. Woodward (later mayor of West Bromwich), his brother-in-law, Mr. Thornton acting as manager for him. He also informs me that during that time the mill was grinding 'Blacking', the coal slack being brought by barge on the adjacent canal, but he was not sure which of the tenants carried on that business. However, the tenancies must have been short, for in 1911 the trustees granted a 14-year lease of, among other properties, the 'water-mill', to Mrs. C. Ginster, who surrendered the tenancy in 1917.[30] So we come to living memory and the end of the use of water power in the Upper Tame valley. Mr. Lester became

tenant in 1947, Mr. Yates, of Delves Hall Farm, Walsall,
being the owner, and was responsible for some of the
dismantling of the machinery.

In 1969 the mill stood in a dilapidated condition with
little to remind us of its former use. The large house
was derelict and only the cottages and a few of the farm
buildings were in use. The approach of the urban sprawl,
the new motorway junction within 50yds. of the buildings
and the threat of the construction of a monster sewage dis-
posal works over the site, suggested there was little chance
of preserving this most interesting relic of a bygone age.

NOTES

1. *Final Concords*, 1567 (*S.H.C.*, XIII, p. 267).
2. M. Willett, *op. cit.*, p. 184.
3. West Bromwich Manorial Rent Roll, 1626.
4. *Ibid.*, 1630.
5. F. W. Hackwood, *Wednesbury Workshops* (1889), p. 50.
6. Birmingham Reference Library, 297298.
7. West Bromwich Manorial Rent Roll, 1649.
8. Hereford County Record Office, F/VI/KG/1 *et seq.*
9. *Ibid.*, F/VI/KG/7.
10. West Bromwich Manorial Court Rolls, 1686 and 1689.
11. Wednesbury Parish Register.
12. M. Willett, *op. cit.*, p. 187.
13. *Ibid.*, p. 198.
14. Bilston Parish Register, 1715-22.
15. Knight's Account Books.
16. Aris's *Birmingham Gazette*, 29 Nov. 1742.
17. Jos. Reeves, *op. cit.*, p. 114.
18. West Bromwich Inclosure Award; Schedule, 1801.
19. West Bromwich Inclosure Award; Map, 1804.
20. *Parson and Bradshaw Directory* (1818).
21. Collection of Smith Deeds, D 58; West Bromwich Reference
Library.
22. *Wrightson's Triennial Directory of Birmingham* (1823).
23. *Pigot's Commercial Directory* (1835).
24. Jos. Reeves, *op. cit.*, p. 114.
25. Smith Deeds, D 58.
26. *White's Staffordshire Directory* (1855).
27. Smith Deeds, D 61.
28. Smith Deeds, D 63.
29. F. W. Hackwood, *Wednesbury Workshops* (1899), p. 21.
30. Estate Duty account J. A. Dorsett (1913); Smith Deeds D 77.

X

FRIAR PARK FORGE

One of the older mills of the area was that which was later to become the Friar Park Forge (009960). It lay to the south side of the stream on a short leat, at some time operating from a small pool but at others direct from the leat.

The mill, or at least the site, together with adjacent land, was bestowed on the Abbey of Hales (Halesowen) by the lord of the manor of West Bromwich probably very early in the 13th century. The gift may have been made by Richard de Marnham, husband of Margery, the daughter of William, son of Guy of Offney, a little later than that of the Sandwell Estates (*q.v.*). It is likely that the Abbey held the mill and lands in perpetual fee farm rather than with absolute title. It seems more than probable that the ownership of this mill and land is the origin of the name 'Friar Park', applied to a greater area at a later date.

In 1224, Geva, widow of Richard fitz William (that is, the grandson of Guy) promoted a number of suits for dower.[1] Among these actions was one against her brother-in-law, William son of William fitz Guy, for a third of five vivaries, a third of 6s. of rent and a third the capital messuage of 'Bromwyz'; one against the Abbot of Bordesley for a third of three acres of land in Bromwich and another against the Abbot of Hales for a third of 25 acres of land and a mill in the same vill.

The abbey, as was the custom, rented out the mill. Margery, widow of Robert the Miller, raised a suit for dower in 1242, suing the Abbot of Hales for a third of a mill, two acres of land and one acre of pasture in 'Bromwic'.[2] The Abbot called Richard, son of William of Bromwic, to warranty. Richard denied the liability, claiming that Robert 'le Muner' had held the mill and land in villeinage and therefore could not endow his wife with the property. The sheriff called for evidence from a panel of local witnesses and having heard the evidence he decided that Robert had held the land freely and that, consequently, Margery was entitled to her dower.

In 1270 Henry the Miller took the Bromwich Mill at the annual rent of 10s., swearing fealty to the Abbot as lord of the manor of Hales.[3] In 1291, the 'Taxacio Ecclesiastica p. Nicholai IV' states, 'Abbas de Hales de dioc. Wigorn habet apud Bromwich in Decan. de Tamworth . . . et habet ibm. unum molend. valet p. ann. Vs.'.[4] This value is comparable with that of 10s. at which the two mills of the Sandwell Priory were assessed.

The Abbey continued to hold the mill until the dissolution.[5] The property then passed to Sir John Dudley, later to become Duke of Northumberland and Earl of Warwick, and holder of the Manor of Walsall. It may well be, though we cannot be certain, that it was at about this time that the mill was converted to a bloom-smithy. The tenant of the mill, stagnum (pool) and adjacent meadows was William Askue, who held it of the said Duke at an annual rental of £3 6s. 8d.[6] Northumberland was attainted of High Treason and executed in 1553, his property being escheated to the Crown. The iron-mill called the 'fryer parke Smythie' the stagnum called 'le Smythie Poole' and two meadows, in the parish of West Bromwich, called 'le Blomesmethie meadowes' passed to Ambrose, Earl of Warwick, from whom John Persehouse the younger, rented it at an annual rent of 12s., which suggests that the smithy had ceased to work.[7] Certainly at the death of Ambrose, in 1592, the mill was stated to be 'altogether ruinous and in decay'. It was then valued, together with the pool, 'in the state they are now in', at no more than 12d. per annum.

It is improbable that it ever revived as a bloom-smithy for, as shown in an earlier chapter, this was the time when the furnace, the finery and the chafery were being developed in this area.

A plan of 'Delves Mill' belonging to Viscount Dudley and Ward, drawn by John Partridge in 1781, shows a mill on the Tame, close to the Fullbrook confluence.[8] The marking of 'sinder banks' suggests the possibility of it being a forge or at least on the site of a former forge. There has been a temptation to name this as a separate mill, and some have placed it on the Fullbrook, though this plan shows it could not have been. It is possible that this was on the site of the old Walsall bloom-smithy, though it seems more probable that this was another name for the Friar Park Forge, since a sketch map of the same year, 1781, marks but one water-mill site and names that 'Fryer Park Blade and Corn Mill'.[9]

We learn that it was a tan-house up to about 1770 and that it was converted to a rolling-mill by Charles Leonard, who operated for about 20 years.[10] He died between 1802 and 1804. On the various editions of Yates's map from 1775 to the 1790s it is marked as a water mill.

Reeves continues with the information that it was converted to an iron forge by a Mr. Elwell but that it had been in ruins for several years at the time of his writing (1836). He neglects to tell us which member of the Elwell family this was. It seems probable that it was worked in conjunction with the Hateley Mills.

There was some diversion of the stream when the Grand Junction railway was constructed about 1840 and though the site was still marked on the later reprints, about 1855-60, of the first edition 1in. O.S. map, it was finally lost with the construction of the Bescot railway sidings.

NOTES

1. *Plea Rolls*, 1224 (*S.H.C.*, vol. IV, pt. 1, pp. 24 and 29).
2. *Plea Rolls*, 1242 (*S.H.C.*, vol. IV, pt. 1, pp. 94-5).
3. Halesowen Manorial Court Rolls, in *Trans. Worcestershire Hist. Soc.*, vol. 1, ed. J. Amphlett.

4. Stebbing Shaw, *op. cit.*, vol. 1, p. xxi.

5. *Fine*, 1539, Rex v. Wm. Taylour, Abbot of Hales (*S.H.C.*, vol. XII, p. 186).

6. P.R.O., Ex. R., 178/2099.

7. *Ibid.*

8. William Salt Library, Stafford, 14/39.

9. Stafford County Record Office; Q/SB, A. 1781.

10. Jos. Reeves, *op. cit.*, p. 113.

XI

THE WALSALL MILLS

In Walsall there were two water mills of which we have any detailed history; the manorial mill (Town Mill or Lord's Mill) (013988) and the New Mills (009974), the former of which is likely to have been the older. We are not to know whether the manorial mill dated back to Domesday times for there are no details whatsoever of Walsall in that record. However other sources take us back to the 12th century. Since the history of these mills is so entwined with that of the Manor of Walsall, it is necessary to have a table of the holders of the manor available. The tables on pp. 74-76 are extracted from Willmore's *History of Walsall*.

In 1159, Henry II bestowed on his servants, Herbert Ruffus, the manor of 'Walesala' and all appurtenances, 'in wood and in plain, in meadows and pastures, in ways and byeways, in water, in mills and in all places'.[1] Ruffus was to pay £4 per annum in lieu of services. Thus, a water corn-mill was part of the estate before the end of the 12th century.

About 1197, the then lord of the manor, William Ruffus, in consideration of a payment of 12 marks of silver by the burgesses, granted them freedom from all customs and services other than tallage (royal impositions or taxations) and pannage (a charge for pasturing the swine in the woods) at acorn time):[2] This was a most important event in the history of the mill for it freed the burgesses from suit to the manorial mill, a freedom which was to have a future significance.

As a result of a suit, about the possession of certain land, against him, William Ruffus the younger appealed to

Henry III, in 1225-6, who granted him a confirmation of the grant to his grandfather by Henry II. This confirmation was couched in much the same terms as the original charter and specifically mentions mills.[3]

After the death of William Ruffus, about 1247, the manor was held in moieties by the Morteyns and the Paynels (Paganels) into which families his sisters had married. It seems probable that about this time, if not before, the second mill was founded, so that there was one in 'Walsall Borough' and the second in 'Walsall Foreign'.

An inquisition post mortem held after the death of William de Morteyn in 1283-4, showed that his moiety of the manor was worth £14 13s. 1½d. per annum of which a mill accounted for 44s. This moiety then passed to Sir Roger de Morteyn, a nephew of the late Sir William. It was about this time that his great-aunt, holder of the other moiety, made a grant to Sir Roger:[4] 'Likewise take notice how Margery la Rouse, lady of the moiety of the Town of Walsall, has granted to Mons. Roger Morteyn and to his heirs and to his assigns, according to her power, a moiety of the profit of each manor, of mines as well as of seacole as of iron and likewise the fishery from the bridge of the Town of Walsale as far as the New Mill'. This declaration is important in showing definitely that there was a new mill at that time and since the old mill was situated at or near to the Town Bridge, then the new mill would be down stream from it, somewhere in the region of the last edifice of that name, the fishery referred to being the mill dam or lade of the new mill. There is a fishery referred to in a deed of 1304-5 as Ladypool.[5] While this might indicate a dedication to the B.V.M., it is possibly an indication that it was constructed by the recently-deceased Margery la Rouse who held the moiety for nearly 60 years from 1247. In the same year Sir Thomas Rouse granted his cousin, Sir Roger Morteyn, 'a certain road to the windmill of Walshale, for a cart and horses at pleasure.[6] This is the first reference to the Walsall windmill and suggests the inadequacy of the water-

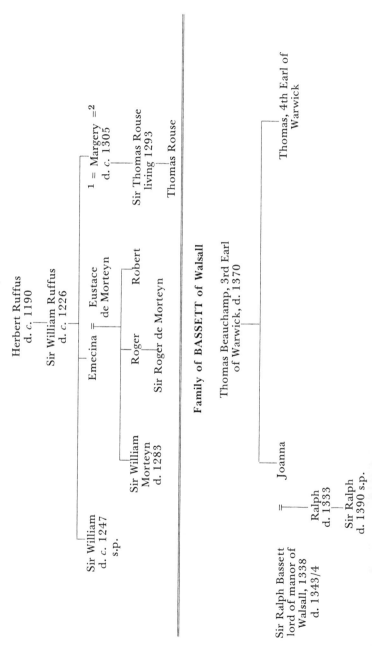

Families of RUFFUS (alias ROUS or ROUSE) and DE MORTEYN of Walsall

Herbert Ruffus
d. c. 1190

Sir William Ruffus
d. c. 1226

Sir William   Emecina = Eustace   1 = Margery = 2
d. c. 1247   de Morteyn   d. c. 1305
s.p.

              Sir William   Roger   Robert   Sir Thomas Rouse
              Morteyn   living 1293
              d. 1283   Sir Roger de Morteyn
                                               Thomas Rouse

Family of BASSETT of Walsall

Thomas Beauchamp, 3rd Earl
of Warwick, d. 1370

              Joanna   Thomas, 4th Earl of
                                                     Warwick
         =
        Ralph
        d. 1333

        Sir Ralph
        d. 1390 s.p.

Sir Ralph Bassett
lord of manor of
Walsall, 1338
d. 1343/4

Families of BEAUCHAMP and NEVILLE, Earls of Warwick and lords of the manor of Walsall

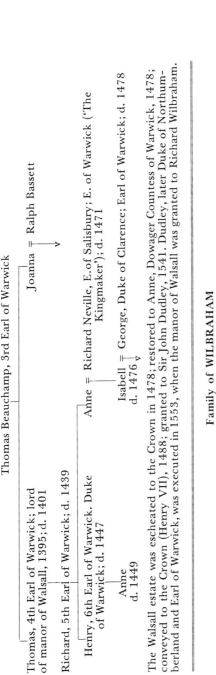

Thomas Beauchamp, 3rd Earl of Warwick

Thomas, 4th Earl of Warwick; lord of manor of Walsall, 1395; d. 1401

Richard, 5th Earl of Warwick; d. 1439

Henry, 6th Earl of Warwick. Duke of Warwick; d. 1447

Anne d. 1449

Joanna = Ralph Bassett

Anne = Richard Neville, E. of Salisbury; E. of Warwick ('The Kingmaker'); d. 1471

Isabell = George, Duke of Clarence; Earl of Warwick; d. 1478
d. 1476

The Walsall estate was escheated to the Crown in 1478; restored to Anne, Dowager Countess of Warwick, 1478; conveyed to the Crown (Henry VII), 1488; granted to Sir John Dudley, 1541. Dudley, later Duke of Northumberland and Earl of Warwick, was executed in 1553, when the manor of Walsall was granted to Richard Wilbraham.

Family of WILBRAHAM

William Wilbraham

Thomas; joint lord of manor of Walsall with his brother; d. 1558

Richard; d. 1558

Thomas; d. 1610

Sir Richard; d. 1643

Elizabeth = Sir Thomas
d. 1705   d. 1692

Mary = Richard Newport

2 da.   2 s.   1. da

**Family of NEWPORT and BRIDGEMAN, Earls of
Bradford; lords of the manor of Walsall**

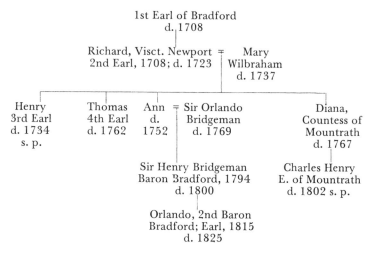

1st Earl of Bradford
d. 1708

Richard, Visct. Newport = Mary
2nd Earl, 1708; d. 1723 | Wilbraham
d. 1737

Henry   Thomas   Ann = Sir Orlando   Diana,
3rd Earl   4th Earl   d.   Bridgeman   Countess of
d. 1734   d. 1762   1752   d. 1769   Mountrath
s. p.   d. 1767

Sir Henry Bridgeman   Charles Henry
Baron Bradford, 1794   E. of Mountrath
d. 1800   d. 1802 s. p.

Orlando, 2nd Baron
Bradford; Earl, 1815
d. 1825

Thomas, the 4th Earl was incapable, and the estate was
administered by Orlando Bridgeman and Diana, Countess of
Mountrath.

Note. — Some of the dates in the above tables taken from
        Willmore, would appear to be suspect.

mills. In the following year, 1305-6, Sir Roger made a
grant of two mills in the fee of Walshale, 'the water-mill
at Bertmescote [Bescot] and the windmill at Waleshale',
to Henry de Prestwood in exchange for a share in a
fishery.[7] It may well be that this was a short-term lease,
for Willmore quotes a deed of 1308-9 (source not given),
which stipulated that the grantee should grind at the
lord's mill for 20 years and not longer.[8]

In the same year, the co-partners in the lordship,
Sir Roger de Morteyn and Sir Thomas Ruffus, for a
consideration, renewed the 1197 charter of Sir William
Ruffus, to the burgesses, this time including freedom from
tallage and pannage and other liberties.[9]

About this time Ralph Bassett of Drayton appears.
He acquired the Morteyn moiety, probably through

unredeemed mortgages in the period 1311-17.[10] In 1317-8,
John, son of Henry de Prestwode, made a grant to Sir
Ralph Bassett of two mills in the fee of 'Walshale'.[11] This
probably indicates a surrender of the lease to the mort-
gager. In 1338, the same Sir Ralph acquired the other
moiety, hitherto the property of Thomas le Rouse[12] and
so reunited the manor under one lordship.

At the death of Sir Ralph Bassett in 1343-4, the
inquisition revealed that the assets of the manor had
been sadly depleted. There is reference to but one water-
mill, the value of which was assessed at 13s. 4d.

That the mills were leased out to corn-millers is born
out by that interesting document of 1396, entitled
'Concerning the grynding of corne, by the Inhabitants of
Walsale at the lord's mill'.[13] The tenant 'Jenkyn Cole of
my lordes Mylle at Walshale' pleaded against the burgesses
of the town that they refused to grind their corn at his
mill, as he said they should, but took it to Rushall and
other mills. The burgesses appeared before the Commissioners and pleaded their exemption from mill-suit on
the ground of the charters granted by the lords of the
manor in 1197 and again in 1308-9. The Commissioners
accepted the evidence of the burgesses and advised
Jenkyn Cole that his best course would be to employ
a new and more skilful miller and do his best to cultivate
the friendship and goodwill of the burgesses.

With the death of the third Sir Ralph, in 1390, the
Bassett tenure came to an end and the manor passed to
a relative by marriage, Thomas Beauchamp, 4th Earl of
Warwick. Walsall remained part of the estates of the
Earls of Warwick for a hundred years, though it is
doubtful if any of them ever visited the town. This
family, so important in the wider pattern of England's
history, with its part in the Wars of the Roses, its
successes and tragedies, its part in the plottings of the
time, needs no account here. Sufficient to say that the
manor was escheated to the Crown about 1476, and
after its temporary return to Anne, Dowager Countess
of Warwick, it was confirmed to Henry VII in 1488.

The overseer of the Warwick estates in 1500, Thomas Goodman, granted a lease for 50 years at an annual rent of £10, to Richard Hopkyns, the Mayor of Walsall and the burgesses of the town and borough of Walsall, except four tenements, the water mill and pond, called the 'Town Myll' and two crofts which were reserved for the King's use.[14] For some unexplained reason, this deed appears under the inaccurate date of 1438 in the Calendar.

Another lease of 1505, granted the Walsall manor, both Borough and Foreign, to John Dyson.[15] This included 'all burgages and lands, all mills etc., court leets etc., and all lands which Roger Dore and Martin Ardern had then lately held'. John Dyson surrendered the lease in 1510 and Robert Riston was appointed bailiff. He was joined as co-bailiff two years later by William Gower. This state of affairs continued for 11 years until 1523, when the King granted a lease of the manor at a rent of £40 per annum to his servants and favourites, Robert Acton and William Gower.

Acton, through his attempts to exact rents, services and tolls, was a most unpopular man in Walsall. In 1524 he preferred a bill in the Court of Star Chamber against Richard Hopkyns (or Hopkys), Richard Bingley (or Dingley), and Nicholas Woodward of Walsall, accusing them, among other things, of inciting the people to revolt, ringing the alarm bell, leading armed processions through the town, riotous assembly, forcibly entering one of his mills.[16] These men undoubtedly were dignitaries of the town, Hopkyns and Dingley each serving terms as mayor.

It continued to be the custom to lease out the mills, which in the 16th century appear to have increased in number, though some inevitably did not long survive. In 1539, Robert Acton leased to George Hawe of Walsall, two mills, one being a water mill and the other a horse mill.[17] The Hawe family at a later date owned the windmill at Caldmore. It is interesting to note the existence in Walsall of a horse mill, one of the few recorded in South Staffordshire. It is an indication of the need to search for sources of power other than water and wind.

On the death of Acton in 1540, the estates were granted by Henry VIII to the Dudley family in whose hands they remained until 1553 when the abortive attempt to place Lady Jane Grey on the throne led to its reversion to the Crown. In the same year, Queen Mary granted the Manor of Walsall to Richard Wilbraham at an annual rent of £40.

During the tenure of his son, Thomas, in 1576, a manorial rent roll was prepared.[18] From this we learn that in the Foreign of Walsall: (a) Thomas Wollaston held a pasture called Newe Mill Meadow, eight acres at 20d. per annum; (b) John Curtys held a pasture called Newe Mille Meadowe, 16 acres at a rent of 20s. 8d. per annum, and a water mill called The Newe Mill at a rent of 33s. 4d. per annum; (c) Richard Worthington held a water mill called the Meadow Mill and the Longe Meadowe, five acres at £5 per annum; (d) John Tyrle held a meadow called Walkemille, two acres with a croft of three acres at an annual rent of 33s. 4d. Within the demesne lands of 'Le Burrowe de Walsall', Thomas Wollaston held the water mill called the Town Mill with an adjoining meadow called the Mill More, two acres, at the annual rent of £3 3s. 4d. The Meadow Mill is one which we have failed to locate so far. The suggestion of a walk-mill (fulling-mill) revives the question of the locality of such a mill that we have met with in the mid-14th century.

A perambulation of 'Boundes, Marches or Limits' of the same date, attached to the above MS. copy, contains references to 'Perkmill Lane' (Peck mill? *q.v.*), a 'Blome Smythie, on the river called Shelfield Broke' (at or near Rushall Mill) and the 'Clockmill', which will be discussed later.

Homeshaw refers to a survey of the manor in 1617 from which he quotes the information that John Wollaston held 'a water mill and meadow adjoining called the Mill More, a pcl of meadow that formerly the ponds of a water mill called Newe Mill, and the ponds of a smithy called an iron mill or smithy now in decay' for which he was assessed at £21 11s. 4d.[19] This survey does not appear to be the same one as that of the same date in the possession of Lord Bradford.[20] The latter, in Latin, contains no mention of the mills themselves, nor of assessment values. It does, however, give the information that,

> John Wollaston holds one arable land in Mill Furlong [below the Town Mill] and two acres of arable in Mill-furlonge formerly belonging to John Pershouse and onetime Sivieter's.
>
> Zena Curteys, widow, holds one pasture called Newe Mill Meadow.
>
> Richard Develey [Deeley?] holds one pasture called Walk-mill Meadow.
>
> John Bennett holds one pasture lying next to Walkmill Bridge.

Other entries appear to refer to the bloom-smithy which will be discussed with the Bescot Mill.

Since the Walkmill Meadow was included with both the Park entries and the Caldmore entries and since there is no reference to such a bridge on the Willenhall brook, part of the Tame or the Fullbrook, in the account of the manorial bounds in the same survey, it appears most probably that this mill lay somewhere between the Town Mill and the New Mill as did the Meadow Mill. This is the last reference we have to either of these mills.

A yet later survey of 1649 contains no direct reference to the mills but mentions land adjacent to both the 'old Mills' and the 'new Mills'.[21] Mention is made of a John Saunsome Baker (name or occupation?) who held certain land 'besides the Mills which are to be rated'.

In 1701, Lady (Elizabeth) Wilbraham, widow, Lady of the manor and last of that name, leased the Old Town Mill to the Mayor and Commonalty for 500 years at an annual rent of 2s., on condition that they should rebuild the mill and use it for the benefit of the poor.[22]   The rent was still being paid in 1887 long after the demolition of the mill.

Between 1685 and 1712 at least, a family named Wiggins were corn-millers and operated a number of mills, both wind and water, in the area from Walsall to Sedgley. John Wiggins, senior, the miller at New Mills, died in July 1712.[23]

Throughout the second half of the 18th and the early 19th centuries, the price of corn and consequently of flour and bread, fluctuated, frequently reaching very high rates, resulting in great hardship for the poverty-stricken workmen and labourers in the growing industrial areas, and nowhere worse than in South Staffordshire. It is little wonder that such conditions led to civil disturbances often directed against the millers and bakers.

In 1756 we see,

> Whereas a malicious set of people did lately assemble together at the Mill of William Woolriche, near the Town, in order to destroy the same; and did prejudice the same Mill and House, which, by what the Inhabitants can learn. it is occasion'd by the Miller's making use of what they call Bolting-Mills, to the prejudice of the Publick; if that should be the Cause of their Grievances, we whose names are subscribed are willing to take down the said Bolting-Mills in our possession, to prevent further such grievances. William Woolrich, Thomas Green, T. Bell, Zach. Twamley, John Mills, John Crutchley.[24]

And again in 1782,

> On Tuesday last, about Eight o'Clock in the morning, upwards of One Hundred Colliers etc. collected together and went to the House of Mr Crowther of Bescott near Walsall and obliged him to sign a written paper, promising to sell Wheat and Malt at Five Shillings a Bushel; and after regaling themselves with his Ale departed. They then waited upon Mr Woolrich, at New Mills and ordered him to sign a paper, expressing that he should not sell Flour for more than Six Shillings per Strike. They then proceeded to Walsall, where they seized a Waggon loaded with Flour, belonging to Mr Webb of Lichfield and after drawing it in a Kind of Triumph through part of the Town and across the Market Place, obliged Mr Webb to sell it at Six Shillings

per Strike, three sacks of which was lost in the distribution.
After this they divided into parties, one of which searched
the houses of several Bakers in the Town etc.[25]

In 1793 the Staffordshire Yeomanry were under severe
pressure when the Borough Justices were congratulated
by Colonel Edward Monkton on the way in which they
had dealt with a threatened attempt to burn a miller
in effigy.[26]

On the death of the 4th Earl of Bradford, grandson of
the above-mentioned Lady Wilbraham, the estate was
divided in 1763 between his sister Diana, Dowager
Countess of Mountrath, and a nephew, Sir Henry Bridgeman.[27] To Lady Diana fell the manor of Walsall, including
certain messuages and tenements, lands, a water mill and
the advowson of the parish church. A manorial survey
of this date, 1763, was accompanied by a map of the
Mountrath properties.[28] On this the Town Mill is marked
as the Old Malt Mill. The only other mill shown is the
New Mill, at that time leased to William Woolrich. The
mill dam is shown as very narrow, a mere widening of
the stream itself. Woolrich also held the three small
fields bounding the 'Mill Pound' and named as the Pool
Pieces.

In 1775 the Corporation of Walsall was still paying a
rent of 2s. per annum for the 'Malt Mill' to the Bradford
estates.[29]

The picture of Walsall drawn about 1796, by the Rev.
Stebbing Shaw, and included in his *History of Staffordshire,* shows the Town Mill. At that time the mill was
coming to the end of its career, and there is no record
of it being worked in the 19th century. Willmore stated
that it was removed about 1813,[30] but when discussing
the 1851 improvements in the bridge area,[31] he stated,
'The first step in the march of improvement was the
removal of the old corn mill, which stood where the
"Observer Buildings" now stand. It had been for several
years occupied as a blacksmith's shop by a person
named Chadwick. The old materials sold for the sum of
£31. The mill was the property of the lord of the manor,

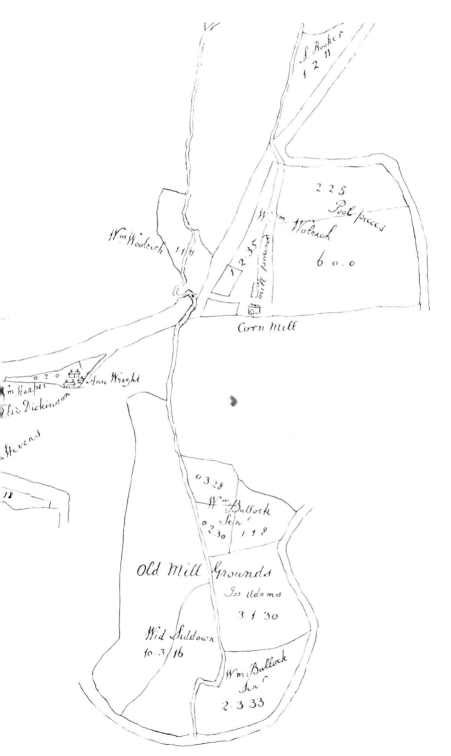

Plan 2: Walsall New Mills. (Mountrath Map, 1763)

and the Corporation still pay the sum of two shillings per annum by way of acknowledgment of his claim. In the front of the mill was a watering place for horses. The mill-race itself was partly covered over at this time, but it was not until 1851 that the remaining portion was finally built over'. In a typed MS., Homeshaw gives the same story about the blacksmith Chadwick, but at the earlier date of 1813.

In the early part of the 19th century the number of corn mills greatly increased in this area. As might be expected, while a few water- and wind-powered mills struggled on for a time, steam power was replacing them. Thomas Pratt, miller, erected a steam-engine for grinding corn in 1812, 'situate at the first navigation bridge on the road from Walsall to Bloxwich'.[32]

However, the New Mills survived for many years. The Jones family, who also worked the Wednesbury Bridge Mill, operated it, residing on the premises. Whitmore Jones, who had occupied it in 1813,[33] was joined by his son about 1828. He died about 1835 and William Jones continued until 1856.[34] Henry Jones then took over until 1879. Then the mill passed into the hands of Henry Boys who occupied it for many years.[35] He brought a successful action against the Corporation of Walsall for impeding the supply of water to the mill. After his death in 1898, the business was carried on by his widow, who was joined by her son Sidney in 1908. It is believed that the mill ceased to operate about 1926 though the family continued to reside on the premises for a number of years, carrying on other businesses. The mill dam was still marked in 1927 on a map in the Walsall *Red Book* of that year.

NOTES

1. Walsall Chartulary, fol. 130; F. W. Willmore, *History of Walsall* 1881), p. 48.
2. Walsall Calendar of Deeds, No. 1.
3. *Plea Roll*, 1225-6; Willmore, *op. cit.*, p. 56.
4. Walsall Chartulary, fol. 138.
5. *Ibid.*, fol. 144; Willmore, *op. cit.*, p. 65.

6. *Ibid.*, fol. 144.
7. *Ibid.*, fol. 132.
8. Willmore, *op. cit.*, p. 79.
9. Walsall Chartulary, fol. 133.
10. *Ibid.*, fol. 132b.
11. *Ibid.*
12. *Ibid.*, fol. 144b.
13. *Ibid.*, fol. 154.
14. Walsall Calendar of Deeds, No. 49.
15. Excheq. Rolls, 1512; Willmore, *op. cit.*, p. 87.
16. Walsall Note Book, p. 174; Walsall Reference Library.
17. Willmore, *op. cit.*, p. 91.
18. MS. copy in the Walsall Reference Library.
19. E. J. Homeshaw, *The Borough and Foreign of Walsall* (1960), p. 33.
20. Weston documents, 1/2; Muniment room, Weston-under-Lizard.
21. Uncatalogued document, No. 53, Walsall Town Chest.
22. Walsall leases, No. 15; Homeshaw, *op. cit.*, p. 84.
23. Wednesbury Parish Register.
24. Aris's *Birmingham Gazette*, 23 August 1756.
25. *Ibid.*, 21 October 1782.
26. Uncatalogued documents, Nos. 190, 191, Walsall Town Chest; Homeshaw, *op. cit.*, p. 96.
27. Willmore, *op cit.*, p. 102
28. Mountrath map (1763), Walsall Central Library.
29. Walsall Rent Roll, 1775; Weston documents 1/2.
30. Willmore, *op. cit.*, p. 79.
31. *Ibid.*, p. 398.
32. Thomas Pearce, *History and Directory of Walsall* (1813).
33. *Ibid.*
34. *Post Office Directory* (1856).
35. W. F. Blane, MS., 'Street Names of Walsall', p. 198

XIII

RUSHALL MILL

In 1086, one Turchill, tenant of William fitz Ansculf, held the manor of 'Rischale', formerly owned by the Saxon, Waga. Part of the property was a mill valued at fourpence. This was the lowest assessment of the value of a mill in this part of the country from which we may assume that it was an insignificant edifice probably serving little beyond the needs of this particular manor, where there were but six villeins and two bordars. This mill situated on the more easterly of the streams of the Walsall Water (or Northern Tame) within a few hundred yards of Rushall Hall (019995), was for much of its time manorial property and as such shared the history of the manor. The descent of the manor of Rushall may be seen from the following table extracted from Willmore's *History of Walsall.*

The mill itself, as may be expected, leaves little direct record. In 1199, the second William of Rushall brought an action against William Ruffus, lord of the manor of Walsall, in respect of the mill and one acre of ground.[1] He failed to appear to pursue the case. This suggests that by some means or other during his nonage the mill and suit had passed out of the control of the 'de Rushalls'. Certainly in 1227 there was still some confusion.[2] Hugh de Bueles (Sir Hugo de Boweles), husband of Alice de Rushall, the surviving member of that family, brought an action against John de Parles for two parts of the mill in Rushale, the rights of his wife. The defendant pleaded that he did not hold the mill in fee but that William de Waleshale held it of him at an annual rent of 18s. Early in the 14th century, in the time of Edward II, Robert 'Molendinarius' (the miller) was one of the witnesses of a

Though there remain no details of this mill for the next two centuries there can be little doubt that it continued to exist and that the same work was carried on there. The next reference is that contained in the Walsall survey of 1617.[4] As previously stated, this document contains no actual reference to the mills themselves, but some of the entries are revealing. The most important in relation to this smithy is the following:

> Ricus Parkes de Willingsworth ten. lib . . . una pastur vocat Smythie leasowe ac. duo prata vocat le Bloome Smythie meadowes nup Levesons & quondam Rudgways.

While this refers to the land only, it is almost certain that the land was attached to the smithy. Richard Parkes of Willingsworth in Wednesbury, was an ironmaster (*see* West Bromwich Old Forge) and controlled the family interests from 1602 to 1619. Sir Walter Leveson had died in 1602. So we learn that the smithy had passed through the hands of Rudgway (Ridgeway?), the Levesons, and finally to the Parkes family.

A certain amount of confusion may arise from the Town Survey and rate assessment of 1617 previously referred to.[5] This, in enumerating the holdings of John Wollaston, includes the ponds of a smithy 'called an iron mill or smithy now in decay'. This might be explained by assuming that it is a reference to some other smithy or that the 'decay' refers to some ponds not now in use by the bloom-smithy. Certainly it would seem improbable that Wollaston held the smithy himself.

We have no other information on this mill other than that Willmore states that 'in making of the present sewage at Bescot, the remains of an ancient ironworks were discovered'.[6]

NOTES

1. *Survey of Walsall Manorial Lands*, 1617; Weston Documents 1/2.
2. Walsall Chartulary, fol. 132.
3. *Ibid.*, fol. 132b.
4. As 1 above.
5. Homeshaw, undated MS.; Walsall Reference Library.
6. Willmore, *op. cit.*, p. 242.

XII

WALSALL BLOOM-SMITHY MILL

Few bloom-smithies have left much trace since, as has already been described, they were essentially small undertakings, often of a temporary nature, usually situated close to their supplies of iron ore and charcoal, and associated with methods which were to become obsolete in the 17th century. The Walsall bloom-smithy was no exception.

It was situated close to where the Walsall branch of the Tame and the Fullbrook joined the main stream (007963), but whether it took its power from one of these tributary streams or from the main river we cannot tell. A description of the 'Bounds of the Mannor of Walsall' in 1617 states that they extended 'from James Bridge descendinge the river there alonge to Bescott Bridge and down along from the same Bridge descendinge the same River unto the Tame Shrubbes and so to the River of Tame and so alonge by the sd. River of Tame untill it meeteth with ffulbrooke water including within this manr. The Meadows there called Tame Shrubbes meadowe and Bloome Smythie Meadowes'.[1] This would seem to be a reasonably explicit as to its location.

The earliest reference that we have to the smithy is contained in the charter of Roger de Morteyn made to Henry de Prestwode of two mills in the fee of 'Walshale'.[2] One was a water mill used for iron at Bertmescote (Bescott) and the other a windmill at Walsall. This charter was dated 1306. Twelve years later there was another charter granted by John, son of Henry de Prestwode, to Sir Ralph Bassett of two mills in the fee of Walsall.[3] While these are not detailed it seems probable that they are the same as the aforementioned.

Early Holders of the Manor of Rushall

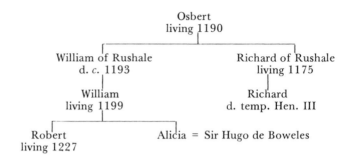

Osbert
living 1190

William of Rushale
d. *c.* 1193

William
living 1199

Richard of Rushale
living 1175

Richard
d. temp. Hen. III

Robert
living 1227

Alicia = Sir Hugo de Boweles

Family of BOWELES of Rushall

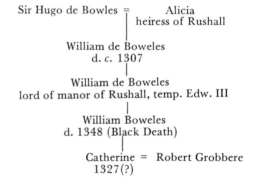

Sir Hugo de Bowles = Alicia
heiress of Rushall

William de Boweles
d. *c.* 1307

William de Boweles
lord of manor of Rushall, temp. Edw. III

William Boweles
d. 1348 (Black Death)

Catherine = Robert Grobbere
1327(?)

Family or GROBBERE of Rushall

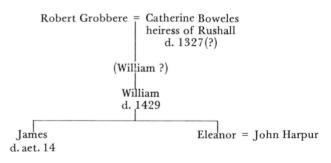

Robert Grobbere = Catherine Boweles
heiress of Rushall
d. 1327(?)

(William ?)

William
d. 1429

James
d. aet. 14

Eleanor = John Harpur

Family of HARPUR of Rushall

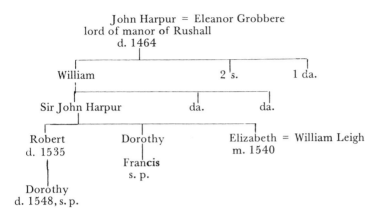

John Harpur = Eleanor Grobbere
lord of manor of Rushall
d. 1464

William   2 s.   1 da.

Sir John Harpur   da.   da.

Robert   Dorothy   Elizabeth = William Leigh
d. 1535   m. 1540

            Francis
            s. p.

Dorothy
d. 1548, s. p.

Family of LEIGH of Rushall

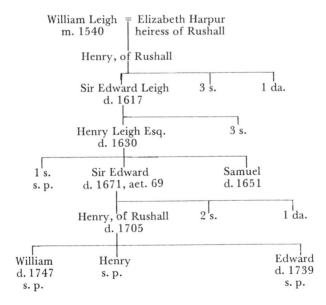

William Leigh = Elizabeth Harpur
m. 1540   heiress of Rushall

Henry, of Rushall

Sir Edward Leigh   3 s.   1 da.
d. 1617

Henry Leigh Esq.   3 s.
d. 1630

1 s.   Sir Edward   Samuel
s. p.   d. 1671, aet. 69   d. 1651

Henry, of Rushall   2 s.   1 da.
d. 1705

William   Henry   Edward
d. 1747   s. p.   d. 1739
s. p.   s. p.

Note.—Several of the dates, quoted above from Willmore, would
appear to be suspect.

conveyance of land in Rushall.[3] This would be during the tenure of the second William de Boweles. The next mention of the mill that we find is in 1339, when William Poul of Rushale made a grant of land stated to be adjacent to the 'regia strata' (King's highway) to Walsall and to the road leading to the mill at Rushale.[4] In 1348 the third William died of the Black Death and the estate passed to his son-in-law, Robert Grobbere. Five years later, in 1353, we find John atte Hurst of Russhale making a grant of land called 'del Bedelscroft' in Russhale to Thomas 'Molendinarius' and Alice his wife.[5] Fourteen years later there was a similar grant by Thomas, son of John atte Hurst of Russhale, to Thomas, son of John le Muleward, living in Ruschal, of lands and tenements in that manor.

The name of an adjacent enclosure, the Mill Hey, occurs in a number of documents. In 1386 John de Sheffel (Shelfield) of Woodende made a grant to Richard de Bloxwyche of land called 'le mulleheye' in Ruschale lying between the lands of William Grobber and of John atte Lynde.[6]

One interesting item, dated 1395, is headed 'Concerning the grynding of corne by the Inhabitants of Walsale at the lord's mill'.[7] In this the tenant of the Walsall Manorial Mill, 'Jenkins Cole, of my lordes mylle at Walshale' complained that the burgesses of the town would not take their corn to his 'mylle' to be ground but preferred to take it to 'Ruysshale Mylne'. As no mill suit was attached to the Walsall mill he lost his casé.

There are further references to the property mentioned in 1386. In 1481 Henry Spourier of Walsale obtained a grant from William Hethe, of a croft called 'le Myllehey' lying in the fee of Russhale,[8] while in 1444, Henry Sporyour, 'lorymer' of Walshale, granted to Roger Sporyour, the croft called 'Mollehey' in the fee of Ruschale.[9]

The Grobbere family held Rushall until the mid-15th century when the last member of that family, Eleanor, was married to John Harpur, who built Rushall church. He died in 1464.

The manor then passed through some four generations of Harpurs, the family finally ending when again the remaining member was a daughter, Elizabeth, who married William Leigh in 1540. It remained in the Leigh family until the beginning of the 19th century.

We find that in 1593 the court 'presente the hyghe way that leadeth from Willenhall and Bentley to Rushall Milne between Walshall Parke and Wombridge forde in the forren of Walshall is not passageable in Winter tyme; is in the decaye of the forren of Walsall and to be repayred by the Inhabitants of the said forren'.[10]

During the Civil Wars, Rushall was a centre of activity. In 1642, Sir Edward Leigh fortified the Hall and held it for the Parliamentarians. A year later it was subjected to attack by a strong Royalist force led by Prince Rupert. On its capture it was garrisoned by royalist troops under the command of Colonel Lane, who came from neighbouring Bentley Hall. The activities of this garrison attracted the attention of the parliamentary forces and in 1644 Colonel Lane surrendered to the Earl of Denbigh. From that time the garrison leader was one Captain Tuthill, a zealous anti-royalist. The Hall was finally dismantled in 1644. Of the fate of the mill during this period we can only guess.

It is probable that this small mill, on its insignificant stream, was converted to the use of the iron industry in the early part of the 17th century. Writing in 1686, Dr. Plot describing the types of iron ore to be found in South Staffordshire, stated that the best type was to be found in the grounds of Mr. Henry Legh of Rushall, in the 'Mill Meddow' near the furnace in the Park.[11] The establishment of a furnace at this time suggests that the stream was used for operating the bellows, as described in an earlier chapter. The mill was probably converted later to a forge or hammer-mill.

Willmore states, without quoting sources, that the furnace was standing in 1718 and a forge stood close by in 1735.[12] In fact in 1788, when John Churchill, the ironmaster of Hints near Lichfield, died, he was the owner of the Rushall furnace, mills and farm.[13] He was not operating them himself for they were out on a lease which had another 17 years to run.

It is probable that its connection with the iron industry ceased about the turn of the century, as was the case of most of the water mills, and that it was re-converted to corn-grinding.

In 1834, Joseph Smith, corn-miller, who lived at Goscote Lodge, was operating the Rushall mill as well as old windmill at Bloxwich.[14] It continued in this business for some years, for in 1855, when it was described as Butt's Mill, it was worked by one William Flower.[15]

By 1885 the site had been occupied by an iron and brass foundry, but a portion of the tail race was still visible.[16]

NOTES

1. *Curia Regis Roll*, 1199; Willmore, *op. cit.*, p. 250.
2. *Plea Roll*, 1227; Willmore, *op. cit.*, p. 225.
3. Walsall Calendar of Deeds, No. 8.
4. *Ibid.*, No. 13.
5. *Ibid.*, No. 19.
6. *Ibid.*, No. 25.
7. Walsall Chartulary, fol. 154.
8. Walsall Calendar of Deeds, No. 45.
9. *Ibid.*, No. 53.
10. *Staffordshire Quarter Session Roll* 1593 (*S.H.C.*, 1930, p. 353).
11. R. Plot, *op. cit.*, p. 159.
12. Willmore, *op. cit.*, p. 242.
13. Aris's *Birmingham Gazette*, 25 April 1788.
14. *White's Staffordshire Directory* (1834).
15. *White's Directory of Birmingham* (1865).
16. 25in. to 1 mile, O.S. map.

COAL (COKE, COE) POOL, GOSCOTE, AND CLOCK
MILLS

The history of these three mills, close together in the Pelsall-Rushall area, is very obscure.

The Clock Mill (011032) was situated on the Clock Mill brook at Pelsall. What was a clock mill? Why the name? Was there a clock displayed on the outside of the building? Did the name originate from the regular beat of a trip-hammer in the forge? It is probable that we shall never know. The earliest reference to it that we have found is in a rent roll of 1576, where in a perambulation of 'The Meres, Bounds, Marches or Limits of the Lordshippe of Walsall' occurs the statement 'ascendynge alsoe by another perle called Clock Mill perle through a meadowe and up by Pelsall and Goscote meadowes unto Clock Mill aforesaid'.[1] A similar document dated 1617, in the possession of Lord Bradford refers to the mill in almost identical terms.[2] The site appears to have become disused by the end of the next century since it is not marked on Yates's map of 1775. The local council have attempted to perpetuate the name by calling a neighbouring street Clockmill Road. An area of marshy ground, shown on the 1884 25in. O.S. plan may well mark the site of a one-time mill dam here.

The origins of the Goscote Mill (022014) are difficult to place unless it be the unnamed bloom-smithy mentioned in the 1576 perambulation (*see* above). If, however, this smithy was actually on the Shelfield brook and not just close to the confluence of that stream and the Clock Mill brook then it follows that the Goscote Mill did not exist at that date and probably not at the 1617 date either. By 1775 the Goscote site is marked but no mill is shown on the Shelfield brook.[3] The Goscote site appears to have been occupied by a forge until the construction of the Goscote Sewage Farm on ground purchased by the Walsall Corporation in December 1904,[4] though the 25in. O.S. plan of 1884 marks a 'Mill House' a few hundred yards lower down stream close to the railway. The bed of the stream itself appears to have been altered, probably when the South Staffordshire Railway was constructed about 1850.

The Coal Pool Mill (018012) was first marked on the 1775 map.[5] It continued to be shown on most maps up to and including the first edition 6in. O.S. map of 1885. It had disappeared by the end of the century. Though it was marked on the map of Walsall included in the 'Walsall Red Book' of that date, we have no knowledge of its use.

NOTES

1. MS. copy of Manorial Rent Roll, 1576; Walsall Reference Library.
2. Weston documents, 1/2.
3. William Yates, *Map of Staffordshire* (1775).
4. Walsall Red Book, 1906, p. 231.
5. Yates, *op. cit.*

XV

BENTLEY MILL

The Bentley Mill (989981) stood north of James Bridge, near the confluence of the Darlaston (or Willenhall) brook and the northern branch of the Tame, being supplied by a lade from the former. While it was one of the less significant mills with an uneventful history, it has the distinction of being one of the very few, the date of whose origin is reasonably certain.

In 1239, Thomas, Lord of Darlaston, granted to William de Bentley, all the watercourse between Darlaston and Bentley, to make a mill upon his land and a mill-pound upon the land of the said Thomas de Darlaston, and to take off as much earth as should be necessary at any time to make or amend the said pool without his enclosure and also he granted him liberty to turn this watercourse wheresoever he pleased between the mill and the place where the two watercourses met; one of which was called Hindebroc and the other Wilnabroc, paying yearly for all services and demands 6d. except for the original.[1]

The mill was constructed and remained in the hands of the Bentley family for at least 40 years. In 1273 letters patent were granted by John, Lord of Bentley, to William Hillory of Bescott and Katherine his wife 'of the Mill of Bentley, with the two pools' etc. However, an inquisition post mortem taken by William de Darlaston, Thomas de Hampstead, William de Wyrley and others, showed that William de Bentley died in 1304, seised of a messuage, one carucate of land with appurtenances in Bentley, valued 40s. per annum, 21s. 7d. of rent of assize and one mill rented at half a mark.[2] It is not certain that this is the same mill.

Henry IV by letters patent in 1408, granted a licence to Nicholas de Ruggeleye and Alianor, his wife, for the sum of four marks to enfeoff John Asheley and Richard Lone of a messuage, a mill, one carucate and a half of land, 12 acres of meadow, three acres of wood and 7s. of rents, with appurtenances in Bentley. This is particularly interesting in that it marks the coming of the Lone or Lane family to Bentley where they were to be for something like 300 years. The most celebrated members of this family were undoubtedly Colonel Lane of Bentley and his sister Jane who gave outstanding support to the royalist cause during the Civil Wars. In 1412, the above-mentioned John Asheley, by charter, granted the same property back to Nicholas Ruggeley.[3]

There follows almost 400 years of silence, until we find it marked on the 1775 map of Yates, as well as in his later editions. For at least part of the 18th century it served as a blade-mill.[4] It was still shown on the first edition of the 1in. O.S. map in 1834 at which date it was still operating as a corn mill. In that year Henry Eld was the corn-miller,[5] but by 1850 the firm of Wright and Underhill had become the millers.[6] On the 1885 edition of the 6in. O.S. map it is marked as 'Bentley Flour Mill'.

The diversion of the streams, due largely to the construction of the M6 motorway, has made identification of the site impossible.

NOTES

1. Stebbing Shaw, *op. cit.*, vol. 2, p. 89.
2. *Ibid.*, p. 93.
3. *Ibid.*, p. 94.
4. Stafford County Record Office; Q/SB A. 1781.
5. *White's Staffordshire Directory* (1834).
6. *Slater's Classified Directory* (1850).

XVI

SPARROW'S FORGE

The family of Sparrow first come to our notice in
Wednesbury in 1730, when Mr. Burslem Sparrow was
paying compensation for the tithe land damaged by the
operation of coal mines he rented in the area.[1] Later he
was partnered by Thomas Tomkys, and the firm of
Tomkys and Sparrow, coalmasters, was a power in the
district for many years.[2]

It must have been about this time that 'Sparrow's
Forge' was established (991967). No suitable site on the
Tame or its tributaries appears to have been available,
so it was constructed where a very small stream crossed
what became Sparrow's Forge Lane, and is now known
as Park Lane, Wednesbury. Lacking sufficient water,
horses were used to supply the driving power. This is not
a unique case of the use of this source of power, for a
deed of 1539 refers to a horse mill in Walsall.[3] However,
this could not have proved very satisfactory, and in
1767 the equipment was sold. It was advertised as follows,

> To be Sold; All the materials of a complete HORSE FORGE,
> either together or separate. For further particulars enquire
> of John Sparrow at Wednesbury.[4]

The forge was then re-erected and a small mill pool
constructed to the west of the road. This pool was still
shown on the Yates map of 1796. The forge was operated
for the rest of the century by the Sparrow family. The
1799 *Terrier* shows Mr. James Sparrow as owner of the
forge,[5] but according to the accompanying map the pool
had already been filled in. Hence the forge could not
have been worked by water power for much more than

30 years and we must assume a steam-engine was used from about 1798.

About 1812-13 Edward Elwell, partnered by a Mr. Edwards, took over the forge and commenced business as edge-tool makers.[6] In 1817, after the death of Edwards, Elwell transferred the work to Wednesbury Forge (*q.v.*).

The forge was acquired by John Crowther, the Wednesbury lawyer, and rented to John Russell who lived at the *Turk's Head* in the High Street. In 1835,[7] he was working the Sparrow's Forge which he later converted to the Sparrow's Forge Foundry.[8]

NOTES

1. *Wednesbury Terrier*, 1730; J. F. Ede, *History of Wednesbury* (1962), p. 117.

2. *Wednesbury Court Roll*, 1750; Ede, *op. cit.*, p. 92; West Bromwich Manorial Rent Rolls, 1746 and 1761.

3. Willmore, *op. cit.*, p. 91.

4. Aris's *Birmingham Gazette*, 27 July 1767.

5. *Wednesbury Terrier*, 1799; Wednesbury Central Library.

6. Chas. E. J. Elwell, *The Iron Elwells* (1964), p. 82

7. Wednesbury Rate Book, 1835.

8. Tithe Redemption Schedule, 1846.

XVII

PECK MILL

No mill in this part of the country presents quite the problem that this one does, for we cannot be certain of its precise location or its use. We have evidence of its existence, yet it does not appear marked as such on any map from Yates's 1775 onwards. We know that the Peck Mill weir was on the Tame near to James Bridge and that the same 'fleam' served both this mill and the Wednesbury Forge.[1] Hence this mill must have been sited (about 998964) between James Bridge and Wednesbury Forge.

The first occurrence of the name is a doubtful one. Attached to a rental of the manor of Walsall, 1576, is an account of the 'Boundes, Marches or Limits of the Lordship'.[2] In this is the statement that the boundary passed 'up a lane called Perkmill (Peckmill?) Lane'. From the context, this must have been near to James Bridge.

The next possible reference is again uncertain: 'On Tuesday last, about Eight o'Clock in the Morning, upwards of One Hundred Colliers etc collected together and went to the House of Mr. Crowther at Bescott near Walsall and obliged him to sign a written paper, promising to sell Wheat and Malt at Five Shillings a Bushel; and after regaling themselves with his Ale departed'.[3] We know that the Crowther family, several members of which were attorneys at Wednesbury, helped finance a variety of undertakings, railways, canals, gasworks, iron mines, and iron works in this area during the next half century. From the above, one at least was interested in a flour mill in the Bescott area. The nearest such to Bescott at that time were the Walsall New Mills (*q.v.*). If then we accept

that it was in the Bescott region, the site we have suggested
for the Peck Mill would appear to be this one mentioned
in the Birmingham paper.

In 1832 a dispute arose between John Crowther, the
then representative of that family, and Edward Elwell,
proprietor of the Wednesbury Forge, over the state of
the old Walsall Road which passed their respective
properties.[4] The mill fleam, which was common to both
undertakings, was another matter for controversy and
on 23 October in the same year, following a meeting
at the *George* Hotel in Walsall, Crowther wrote to Elwell,
'a good deal was said as to the level between the Forge
and Peck Mills without arriving at any satisfactory
conclusion. As I am desirous of ascertaining that fact
I will thank you to inform me by bearer whether you
will allow surveyors to come on your property for the
purpose above'.[5] The antagonism continued, and in 1835
Crowther took legal proceedings with inconclusive results.
In the following year he penned this curt missive, 'Mr.
Crowther's compliments to Mr. Elwell and requests the
favour of an interview with him at Peck Mill Weir on
Monday or Tuesday next at any hour Mr. Elwell will
appoint'.[6] The bitterness between the two did not diminish
with the passage of time. In March 1840, in reply to a
request from Elwell, Crowther replied, 'The Peck Mill
Weir is not "rebuilt and replaced in a proper and workman-
like manner" and my applications to you to alter it for
my convenience have been ineffective. I cannot consent
to any alteration even for a temporary purpose for your
accommodation'.

The 1846 Tithe map of Wednesbury shows a small
building at the head of the northern of the two dams
belonging to the Wednesbury Forge. It is close to the
Walsall Road and appears to have water connection
with both river and leat. A small field adjacent is named
in the relevant schedule as belonging to Mr. J. Crowther.
It seems most probable that this was the mill, though
nowhere is it named as such.

The animosity was to continue even after the death of John Crowther, for in 1861 Elwell sued his son, William Crowther and his tenant Samuel Mills for interrupting the flow of the fleam by their working of ironstone. It was ordered that the mining should be conducted in such a way as not to interfere with the supply of water to the forge. A sketch map apparently prepared for this case but now separated from the rest of the papers, is headed 'Peck Mill, Wednesbury, 1861'.[7] It shows the Tame, the mill-race, the L.N.W. railway, and the Wednesbury to Walsall road, but strangely enough does not show the position of the mill. Perhaps this is an indication that the mill had ceased to exist by that date. It is even more strange that it is not marked on Yates's maps of 1775 and 1798, Dawson's map of 1816, the first edition 1in. O.S. map of 1834 nor the 1799 parish map of Wednesbury.

It is a thoroughly unsatisfactory mill from our point of view.

NOTES

1. Elwell, *op. cit.*, p. 87.
2. Walsall Manorial Rent Roll, 1576; MS. copy, Walsall Reference Library.
3. Aris's *Birmingham Gazette*, 21 October 1782.
4. Elwell, *op. cit.*, p. 87.
5. Crowther's Letter Book, Wednesbury Central Library.
6. *Ibid.*
7. MS. in Tipton Central Library.

XVIII

THE WEDNESBURY MILLS

Wednesbury was one of the few places in this area to possess a mill in Domesday times, 'Ibi molim. de ii sol'. Compared with mills in more prosperous parts of the country it was small and unimportant. Its annual value was given as 2s. Yet no doubt it was adequate, not only for the needs of the manor of Wednesbury, but to provide for adjacent holdings such as West Bromwich which had no mill at that time.

The exact location of the manorial mill of Wednesbury cannot be established with complete certainty and consequently a certain amount of confusion in the continuity of the story of at least two of the mills may have arisen. The discrepancies which the reader will find between this present account and the work of other writers arises from the attempts to identify locations from personal knowledge of local topography and from varying interpretations of somewhat ambiguous medieval documents.

In order to understand the problem it will be necessary to study the map of the area: Yates's map will serve the purpose. It will be seen that there were three route crossings of this part of the river; the first a route going southwards from Wednesbury (989942), the second going east-south-east from Wednesbury (988944), and the third going south-east from Wood Green (000945). To give them their present-day names they are Wednesbury Bridge, Hydes Road and Crankhall Lane respectively. The position of the mills may be related to these crossings. It may be of interest to note that the 1799 map of Wednesbury shows a pedestrian or pack-horse bridge with a vehicular ford alongside at both Wednesbury Bridge and Hydes Road while at Crankhall Lane there appears to be a ford only. It is recognised of course that this is not necessarily the state of affairs four or five hundred years earlier.

The second point for consideration is the local topography, which cannot easily be appreciated from a map but which is immediately evident on an inspection of the sites. The Wednesbury Bridge route took advantage of the narrowing of the valley caused by the proximity of the steeper slopes of the Wednesbury Hill and Holloway Bank. Here the route would have to cross less ground subject to flooding than anywhere else in the valley. At the same time a small local 'nick point' provides for an increase in the velocity of the stream. As a contrast, the other two routes cross in each case a broad flat area of at least half a mile wide. While, as is shown by the sites of other mills on the Tame, this is not an insuperable obstacle, it is clear that the Wednesbury Bridge site would be by far the most suitable of the three sites for the construction of a water mill.

The third matter to be decided is the exact location of 'Finchpath' or 'Fynchespath' and the 'Wistie'. Hackwood asserts, without supporting evidence, that 'in Hydes Lane was Finchpath Bridge'.[1] Mr. Ede seems to accept Hackwood's assertion[2] and further suggests that 'Wysti' was a corruption of 'Mesty' (in Wednesbury) and would place 'Wysti Bridge' in Crankhall Lane.[3] These are conclusions which I suggest are misplaced. Willetts quotes a considerable number of documents in which, as well as in the West Bromwich Manorial Court Rolls, there are numerous references to Finchpath, in a variety of spellings, and, more important, to tenements, fields or localities 'in Fynchpath'.[4] Many of these can be located today and appear to cover an area on each side of the present Wednesbury-Birmingham road from the foot of Holloway Bank (989941) to (995923) extending, in places, to about 700yds. to the west, including Harvilles Hawthorne and Black Lake, but to only about 200yds. east of the road. Nowhere is Hately Heath (000936) referred to as being in Finchpath. This is strong evidence that

'Fynchpath' never extended to the Hydes Road area. This we take to indicate that Finchpath Bridge was situated on the site of the present Wednesbury Bridge. The word 'wist' is old English for provisions (food) or the ground on which it was grown. From 1597 to the present day, an area of ground to the south of the West Bromwich Manor, part of the former demesne, has been known as the Wisty (Wistie, Wisti).[5] This was about half a mile from the Hydes Road river crossing, while the Crankhall Lane crossing would be almost a mile from this area. It would be more reasonable to assume that 'Wistibridge' would be at Hydes Road than at Crankhall Lane. The 'Mesty' in Wednesbury was almost equidistant from the two crossings.

From the above, we draw the conclusion that 'Fynch-pathbridge' was the name given to a bridge at the site now occupied by Wednesbury Bridge and that 'Wistibridge' was situated on what is now Hydes Road. These conclusions simplify some of the problems of mill location, but regrettably not all.

Wednesbury Manorial Mill

Our first indication of the existence of this mill, as stated above, is in the Domesday record that it was worth 2s.

Some 145 years later, *c.* 1230, William de Heronville, the then lord of the manor of Wednesbury, 'pro salute animae meae et Aliciae uxoris meae' demised the Wednesbury manorial mill with the accompanying mill suit, to the abbot and monks of Bordesley in Warwickshire in perpetual fee farm, at an annual rent of 10s.[6] He also granted the watercourse which was between the two bridges, the one called 'Wynchespathebrigge' and the other 'Wysti-brigge', 'ad molendinum faciendum apud Wisti' (to the mill made at Wistie). This would appear to be explicit; that the mill was at the Hydes Road crossing. There are several other points of interest in this document. It was envisaged that the mill would serve a much greater area than just Wednesbury for it was stipulated that Wednesbury men should be employed for carrying the meal within the county, but beyond that the monks must make other arrangements for transport. Moreover, the monks could call on every man in Wednesbury to contribute one day's labour per annum for the repair and maintenance of the mill and pool. Permission was also given to the monks to move the mill if they so wished to any other site on the same ground and to carry out any necessary alteration and re-direction of the watercourse between 'the head of the bridge and the ford'. This is not clear. Which bridge? Does it refer to a ford at the Crankhall Lane crossing? If so, this must refer to the mill 'tail race', which would appear to be unnecessarily long.

The Abbey of Bordesley did not retain the operation of the mill but transferred it to one Nicholas de Bordesley, who in turn surrendered it to the Hillary family of Bescot.[7] Meanwhile the Heronvilles and the inhabitants of Wednesbury had withdrawn their suit to this mill, that is, they had neglected to observe the compulsory grinding of the local corn at the mill, without which the structure was of little value. This may have been due to excessive levies charged on the corn ground there, causing the populace to resort to hand mills or even possibly to a later Heronville having constructed a rival mill. In 1287, Thomas Hillary appeared against John de Heronville in a plea that he (John) and his villeins of Wodensburi should do suit to his mill of *Fynchespath* as they used to do.[8] Here we note that the mill is said to be at Finchpath rather than Wistie. Does this indicate that the name Finchpath did include the Hydes Road area at that time, or, what we would claim to be more likely, that the monks had exercised their rights, granted originally, to re-locate the mill in the more favourable position. In 1289 an assize found that Roger, son of Roger Illary, and father of William and Thomas Illary had died seised of a mill and land in 'Wednesburi', which 'Thomas holds' but William should be the rightful holder.[9] In 1315 William Hillary, in his turn, sued 21 inhabitants of Wednesbury that they should do suit to his 'mill of

Fynchspad; in Fynchespad',[10] while in 1352 we find
Roger Hillary, knight, bringing a similar case for his
mill in Wednesbury.[11] There can be no doubt that the
'Wednesbury Mill' was one and the same as the 'Fynchpath
Mill' at that time. Willetts quotes three undated documents
which appear to be relevant here.[12] By their signatories
and the names of the witnesses, these deeds relate to a
period at the end of the 13th century. They are conveyances of property in Finchpath, apparently at the foot
of Holloway Bank and contain reference to the road
to Finchpath Bridge. Among the names contained are
those of William the Miller, and Simon the Miller, who
owned a house at the 'boundary gate', that is, on the
road next to the bridge. It would seem most probable
that they were working a mill at that site and that the
Wednesbury Mill was held by the Hillary family. Had the
Heronvilles, lords of the manor of Wednesbury, erected
a rival mill? Of that we have no evidence. Hackwood
suggests that they had.[13]

This mill remained the property of the abbey until
its dissolution in 1538 when its value was stated to be
20s. per annum.[14]

So far we have considered something of the history of a
manorial corn mill which originated on the Hydes Road
site and was later transferred to Wednesbury Bridge.
From this point we must study the two sites separately.

Hydes Road (Wisty) Mill

We have speculated above as to the possibility of the
simultaneous existence of two mills, one at Wednesbury
Bridge and the other at the Hydes Road site. The inquisition post mortem of the effects of John Heronville in
1315 shows him seised of a water mill and fish pond
valued 6s. 8d.[15] The assignment of dower of Juliana,
widow of John, in 1315, allots to her, one-third of the
value of the mill, while the inquisition of Henry, son of
John, in 1316, shows him possessed of two-thirds of the
mill.[16] Ede points out that a fee farm rent was often

fixed at one-third of the annual value of the property.[17] We have seen above that the value of the manorial mill of the abbey was assessed at 20s. which would bring a rent to the Heronvilles of 6s. 8d. Mr. Ede uses this as an argument against a two mill theory. If this is so, it would seem that this 1315 mill of the Heronvilles was the one operated by the Hillarys at Wednesbury Bridge and was not on the old original site at the Wisty, though that remains a possibility.

By 1423 there was a fulling-mill in Wednesbury[18] and Mr. Ede was of the opinion that this was on the site of the old manorial corn mill at Hydes Road.[19] This theory is supported by the lease for 31 years, granted March 1665 by Brome Whorwood to George Jesson of certain land, including 'half of Walkmillford Meadow'.[20] This lease is reasonably explicit in its definition of locality. It is interesting to note that the former 'Wysti' bridge, probably no more than a small wooden pedestrian bridge, had been replaced by a ford. As late as 1837, John Wood's map of West Bromwich indicates a ford on Hydes Road, though there was a footbridge in 1799.

In 1685 the jury testified 'that the brook or watercourse from the bridge called Wednesbury Bridge towards Walkmill foard is in need of scouring to the detriment of the watermills of the lord aforesaid, called Wednesbury Mills, and that the same brook or watercourse for so much of it lies within this Manor of West Bromwich should be scoured by the owners and occupiers of the lands adjacent to the same brook or watercourse'.[21] This does not tell us whether the mill was still working as a fulling-mill. The import of the order to the inhabitants of West Bromwich will be better understood when it is remembered that the Sheltons, lords of the manor of West Bromwich, also held the manor of Wednesbury at that time.

This mill is one example of two fulling-mills on the Upper Tame in medieval times.[22] This, as is usual with a manorial mill, left little record other than that it existed for more than 250 years. We do not know when it ceased to operate nor have we any trace of it since the end of the 17th century. It seems unlikely that it ever became involved in the iron industry.

Wednesbury Bridge Mill

We have traced the early history of a corn mill on this site up to the dissolution of Bordesley Abbey in 1538. From that date it may have fallen into disuse or passed into other hands. We have no knowledge of it for the next 170 years, but if it followed the pattern of many of the neighbouring mills, it is probable that it was converted to the use of the iron industry towards the end of the 16th century.

In that part of this work dealing with the Wednesbury Forge, there is reference to an attack on the forge in 1597, the result of the disputes between the Parkes of Wednesbury and the Whorwoods of Sandwell. While we have assumed that this incident occurred at the forge at Wood Green, we cannot ignore the possibility that it was at the Wednesbury Bridge Mill, for, at that time and throughout the 17th century, the Whorwoods owned the adjacent riparian meadows on the West Bromwich side from Wednesbury Bridge down to the Hydes Road crossing. Whether or not this incident occurred at Wednesbury Bridge, a forge existed there half a century later. Hackwood describing the mill, stated that 'internal evidence seems to show that it was built in the 17th or 18th century for an iron forge . . . The woodwork is of hewn oak and the ironwork is a fine specimen of the durable cold-blast charcoal iron of olden Wednesbury'.[23]

In 1710, one William Webb is described as of Wednesbury Mills,[24] but whether it is of this site or whether the fulling-mill still existed at this date cannot be determined.

The next occupant of the Wednesbury Bridge Forge of whom we know was John Wood, son of William Wood of Wolverhampton, who made a fortune as contractor for the making of Irish coinage: 'Wood's halfpence'.[25] He first appears as a purchaser of iron from the Aston Furnace in 1753-4[26] and continued to buy iron from both Aston and Hales until 1764-5. The non-appearance of his name from that time may be due to the way in which the accounts were kept and that only the annual summaries survive. In addition to bar iron, he used scrap to produce high quality iron, since scrap was available in increasing quantities.[27] Wood died in 1779 and was buried in Wednesbury.

The name of his successor does not appear to have survived, but in 1816 the mill was offered for sale.[28] It was described as having a 'lift hammer and a tilt hammer in good repair, well adapted for making best and common iron; also sufficient warehouses for storing of scrap iron and manufactured iron'.

However, its days as part of the iron industry were over and it was re-converted to a corn mill. In 1818, Whitmore Jones was listed as corn-miller and coalmaster at Wednesbury Bridge.[29] By 1829 he had been joined by his son in the business.[30] The Jones family continued to operate the mill until 1855: William Jones, 1835-40; Henry, 1840-45; William, 1845-50.

The next millers at Wednesbury Bridge Mill were Hatton Brothers and Caddick.[31] At this time a new mill, operated by steam, was erected on the opposite side of the road to concentrate on the production of flour, while the old side continued grinding pig meal, using an old steam-engine to augment the water power.[32] In 1865 Caddick was replaced by Marsh.[33] The partnership dissolved in 1870 and Joseph Wilkes Marsh became the sole proprietor until it finally closed in 1885, unable to face the competition.[34]

NOTES

1. F. W. Hackwood, *Wednesbury, Ancient and Modern* (1902), p. 31.
2. J. F. Ede, *History of Wednesbury* (1962), p. 108.
3. Mr. Ede appears to have changed his views to some extent in his *Corrigenda*, published by The Black Country Society (1969).
4. Willett, *op. cit.*, pp. 164-224.
5. West Bromwich Manorial Court Roll, 1597,
6. *Plea Rolls, c.* 1230 (*S.H.C.*, vol. IV, pt. 1, p. 170).
7. *Plea Rolls, c.* 1280 (*S.H.C.*, vol. VI. pt. 1, p. 169).

8. *Plea Rolls*, 1287 (*S.H.C.*, vol. VI, pt. 1, p. 165).
9. *Ibid.*
10. *Plea Rolls*, 1315 (*S.H.C.*, vol. IX, p. 55).
11. *Plea Rolls*, 1352 (*S.H.C.*, vol. XII, p. 103).
12. Willett, *op. cit.*, pp. 204-5.
13. F. W. Hackwood, *Wednesbury, Ancient and Modern* (1902), p. 33.
14. *Fine*, 1538 (*S.H.C.*, vol. XII, p. 186).
15. *Inq. P.M.*, 1315 (*S.H.C.*, 1911, pp. 319-323).
16. *Inq., P.M.*, 1316 (*S.H.C.*, 1911, pp. 331-2).
17. Ede, *op. cit.*, p. 24.
18. William Salt Library, Stafford; MS. 28.
19. Ede, *op. cit.*, p. 131.
20. Jesson Deeds, No. 23.
21. West Bromwich Manorial Court Roll, 1685.
22. R. A. Pelham, *V.C.H.*, *Warws.*, vol. 7 (1964), p. 253.
23. F. W. Hackwood, *Wednesbury, Ancient and Modern* (1902), p. 68.
24. Wednesbury Parish Register.
25. Ede, *op. cit.*, p. 132.
26. Knight's Account Books.
27. F. W. Hackwood, *Newspaper Cuttings No. 4;* Wednesbury Central Library.
28. Aris's *Birmingham Gazette,* 19 February 1816.
29. *Parson and Bradshaw Directory* (1818).
30. *Pigot's Commercial Directory of Birmingham* (1829).
31. *Post Office Directory* (1856).
32. F. W. Hackwood, *Wednesbury, Ancient and Modern* (1902), p. 36.
33. *Post Office Directory of Birmingham* (1865).
34. As 32 above.

XIX

WEDNESBURY FORGE

Wednesbury was one of the earliest areas in the Midlands to be worked for iron. Among the properties detailed in the assignment of dower of Juliana Heronville, 1315, was an iron mine, valued at 2s.[1] From then until the end of the 16th century the iron was worked at small bloomeries using charcoal, a process which had almost denuded the Wednesbury area of timber by the early 16th century. This caused the drift of the industry to the Cannock area.[2] By the end of the century the use of water power to operate furnaces, fineries and chaferies brought the development of the various sites from Wednesbury down to Perry Barr. The two chief developers were Thomas Parkes, described as yeoman of Wednesbury, and William Whorwood of Sandwell Hall in West Bromwich. About 1590 Whorwood obtained from William Comberford, lord of the manor of Wednesbury, the lease of a moiety of a forge in Wednesbury. It has been suggested that this was on the site at Wood Green, later known as Wednesbury Forge.[3] While this is probable, though we do not know the exact date of the construction of this forge, we cannot ignore the possibility that it was the Wednesbury Bridge Mill.

It is obvious that there was considerable rivalry between Parkes and Whorwood, a rivalry which culminated in July 1597 in a series of attacks on each others operations.[4] On 18 July, Thomas Parkes and others broke the 'moiety of a Smithy for the making of iron at Wednesbury, property of William Comberford, and expelled William Whorwood the farmer thereof'. At that time Blaise Uyntam was described as the 'finer' and William Heeley was the 'hammerman'.

Wednesbury Forge (002962), situated at the confluence of the southern branch of the Tame and the Willenhall brook, had the advantage of two sources of water supply. It was in a particularly broad, flat area of the valley, which may account for its relatively late construction. If the Parkes-Whorwood affair did occur at this site, the forge was probably built about 1590.

In 1606 William Comberford leased his forge for 21 years to his son-in-law, Walter Coleman of Cannock.[5] It was described then as a forge with finery and chafery, in a 'decayed' state, furnished with a supply of water from dammed watercourses with floodgates. Coleman was to reinstate the forge and pay an annual rent of £20, giving him sole use of the water. He could reduce his rent to £5 13s. 4d. per annum on giving 12 months' notice, but in that case the use of the water would be limited by demands on it by Comberford who proposed to build other mills. This eventually led to a court case, in which Thomas Chetwynd, partner of Coleman, claimed that he had carried out the terms of the lease. Among the works undertaken by Chetwynd, was the construction of a 'weere or stank' on an old watercourse running from James Bridge to 'Brescott' Bridge (on the Wednesbury to Walsall road) to a forge,[6] in other words, the making of the northern mill lade to the Wednesbury Forge. Nothing is known of the fate of the mill on the expiration of the Coleman lease.

In 1656 John Comberford settled the manor on trustees, the settlement containing reference to a forge as part of the estate,[7] yet the will of John Comberford. 1657, records the selling of his ironworks in Wednesbury to John Shelton of West Bromwich.

It was probably about this time (1657) that the forge was leased by John Shelton to Thomas Foley, the mill thus becoming part of the 'Foley empire'. Ten years later it was divided among Thomas Foley's sons, the Wednesbury Forge being included in the Stour valley complex. Two years later, 1669, Walter Needham and his wife, Elizabeth, widow of the late John Shelton, granted a 21-year lease to Philip Foley of several establishments including Wednesbury Forge (*see* West Bromwich Forge).[8] In 1677, Edward Mountford granted to Thomas Foley, three years before his death, the lease, quoted above, of the leat 'to the forge, formerly Thomas Foley's, now Philip Foley's, called Wednesbury Forge'.[9]

In 1676, an agreement was drawn up between Philip Foley and Humphrey Jennens of Earlington (Erdington?), Warwickshire, whereby Foley transferred to Jennens the unexpired portion of the leases of several of the Stour valley properties (*see* West Bromwich Forge), including the Wednesbury Forge. These Jennens operated until about 1690-1. Foley continued an overall control as is shown by his undertaking repairs in 1678, and by an agreement between him and Jennens in 1679.[10]

For the six years 1667-72 inclusive, the output from the Wednesbury Forge varied from 92½ to 141 tons in the year, almost all of it going to the Bustleholme slitting-mill.

From at least 1667 to 1672 the forge was managed by William Spencer, along with West Bromwich and Little Aston forges, on Foley's behalf. During the Foley and Jennens period, Nicholas Record was the hammerman (1672-85), William Whiston was the finer in 1679, and Ishmael Bomford, a labourer at the forge from 1680 to 1684.[11] Other names connected with the establishment in this period were Richard Seamore, 1674; Roger Brisburn, 1687-9; Joshua Spurr, 1693-6; and Thomas Lowe, 1697-8.

Again we do not know the exact date at which the Foley interest came to an end. Professor Johnson states that John Jennens was operating a forge in Wednesbury at the end of the 17th century,[12] but it is possible that this would be the one at Wednesbury Bridge.[13] Certainly the Foleys had departed by 1708. It remains a question whether Brisburn, Spurr and Lowe worked for Foley or Jennens, or operated as forgemen on their own account.

When Richard Shelton leased a moiety of his Wednesbury mines to Richard Parkes in 1708, he was stated to own 'the iron mill commonly called Wednesbury Forge'.[14] The occupant was John Willetts who had been there from at least January 1704,[15] and the mill 'now used for plateing', that is, a rolling-mill. Roger Colley, 1707, and Joseph Beeche, 1708, were forgemen in this period.[16] The Willetts family continued in occupancy for over a hundred years. John Willetts died in 1722 and the forge was taken over by his son, another John, then aged twenty.[17] In 1726 John Willetts, a saw-maker, was one of the trustees appointed on the passing of the Act for the turnpiking of certain local roads.[18] In 1740, Thomas Kester, and in 1742, Jonah Davis were working at the forge.[19] In 1753 John Willetts (II) died. 'He was the proprietor of Wednesbury old Forge and had carried on a very extensive Trade as well to his Advantage as also to ye service of ye Parish in general'.[20]

The forge was the scene of a tragedy in 1758. A boy, named William Toms, 'fell into Mr. Willetts's Forge Pool as he was playing by ye side thereof and was drowned'.[21]

By 1767 a Benjamin Willetts was operating the forge which at that time had a 'south pool' on the Tame.[22] This Benjamin died in 1786 and his successor was another Benjamin. At the end of the century the south pool became known as 'Mrs. Willetts Pool', since Mrs. Benjamin Willetts, widow, carried on the family business after the death of her husband in 1794.[23]

During this period the firm took on a partnership and was known as Holden and Willetts. The saw-making of earlier period gave way to the grinding of gun-barrels.[24] We are told that they used two grindstones for this purpose. It is possible that grinding had been carried on at this factory at a much earlier date, being adapted to the gun trade at the end of the century. In 1767, Joseph Stevens was 'killed by the breaking of a Stone on which he was grinding tools at a Grinding Mill';[25] Wednesbury Forge? The gun trade was nothing new to Wednesbury, for gun-locks had been a principle manufacture here as well as Wolverhampton and Darlaston, for almost a century, though most of the barrel-making and final assembly was a Birmingham trade.[26] Undoubtedly the Napoleonic wars gave impetus to this trade up to 1815.

In 1817, Edward Elwell, soon after the death of his partner, a Mr. Edwards, with whom he had carried on business as a manufacturer of edge tools at Sparrow's Forge, obtained the lease of the Wednesbury Forge.[27] It was then that the great chimney stack, so long a feature of the works, was erected.[28] In 1831 Elwell purchased the premises which at that time consisted of 'a forge or iron mill, also a grinding mill which had formerly been a windmill', 'a house, thirteen cottages which had been workshops, but which Edward Elwell had reconverted into dwellings, together with adjacent land, a forge pool and a watercourse to feed it'.[29] It will be noticed that only one pool existed at this time, the southern pool having been drained for some reason. There were, however, problems in maintaining an adequate head of water. The mill fleam, or leat, which fed the northern pool with water from the Willenhall brook, also served the Peck Mill.[30] As might be expected, disputes arose between Elwell and John Crowther, proprietor of the Peck Mill, both over water rights and the state of the common access roads.[31] The antagonism grew to such proportions that it became public property in 1834 and it would appear that, as a result of a legal suit, Elwell was directed to rebuild the Peck mill weir, which he neglected to do for at least five years.

Edward Elwell, in 1839, was advertising himself as a maker of spades, shovels, hoes and edge tools.[32]

The construction of the South Staffordshire railway in 1850, might well have brought an end to the use of the site but for the necessity of it crossing the adjacent Grand Junction line built a dozen years before. The problem was solved by carrying the newcomer on a wooden viaduct, which avoided the forge and crossed the upper pool. In 1859 an interesting accident occurred: a goods train ran off the rails on top of the viaduct and fell into the north pool. A photograph is to be found in Wednesbury Library.

Sometime before 1851 Edward Elwell handed over control to his only son, Edward Elwell (II).[33] Business continued to expand and though steam power was used, it was to supplement rather than to replace water power. In order to increase this power, the 'new pool' was constructed on the site of the former 'Mrs. Willetts Pool' and was completed in 1855.[34] On the death of his son in 1857, Edward senior resumed the running of the business until his death in 1869.[35] At about the time of Edward II's death they were employing about 300 hands.[36] There was still trouble about the water supply to the north pool and in 1861 the old man brought an action against William Crowther, son of the late John, and his tenant Samuel Mills, accusing them of interrupting the flow of the mill fleam by their ironstone workings.[37] Damages were not awarded but it was ordered that there should be no further interruption.

After the death of Edward senior in 1869, the management passed to his grandson, Alfred. The business continued to thrive in a period of colonial expansion in the next 20 years, though in 1889, only 200 workpeople were employed,[38] this being probably due to increased efficiency of the machinery. Hackwood, writing in 1889, gives us the following interesting information: 'more water wheels were added and the place grew, so also was steam power added, until at the present time, nearly the whole of the machinery can be driven with steam and water jointly, or, in the time of rainy weather when there is a good supply of water, independently of each other. The two pools cover nearly 25 acres and feed five large breast water wheels which are also connected with steam engines of 200 horsepower. The plant includes steam, trip and tilt hammers all of the most approved type'.[39] Though the catalogue of this time lists nearly 1,200 items, spades, shovels, hoes, adzes, billhooks and forks were still the principle products.

After the death of Alfred Elwell in 1902, the firm became a private limited company, as Edward Elwell

Ltd.,[40] and later there followed a number of amalgamations and 'take-overs'.

Water power ceased to be used early in the 20th century, a turbine being installed in 1904. The pools were filled in after the First World War[41] and in 1969 the site of the north pool was a football pitch, while the new pool site is disappearing under the encroachment of a council house estate.

NOTES

1. *Inq. P.M.*, 1315 (*S. H. C.*, 1911, p. 321-3).
2. B. L. C. Johnson, *Charcoal Iron Trade*, 1690-1720; unpublished MS., Birmingham University.
3. Ede, *op. cit.*, p. 124.
4. *Staffordshire Quarter Session Rolls*, 1597 (*S.H.C.*, 1932, pp. 297-300.
5. P.R.O., C2, Jas. I/C 16/41; Ede, *op. cit.*, p. 125.
6. Hereford County Record Office; F/VI/KG/1 *et. seq.*
7. F. W. Hackwood, *Wednesbury, Ancient and Modern* (1902), p. 68.
8. As 6 above.
9. *Ibid.*
10. Hereford County Record Office. F/VI/KG/8.
11. Wednesbury Parish Registers.
12. B. L. C. Johnson, *op. cit.*, p. 145.
13. Ede, *op. cit.*, p. 128, footnote 159.
14. Wednesbury Leases, 1708 and 1710; copy at Wednesbury Town Hall; Ede, *op. cit.*, p. 126.
15. Wednesbury Parish Registers.
16. *Ibid.*
17. *Ibid.*
18. F. W. Hackwood, *Wednesbury Workshops* (1889), p. 80.
19. Wednesbury Parish Registers.
20. *Ibid.*
21. *Ibid.*
22. Burr map, 1767; MS., Wednesbury Central Library.
23. *Wednesbury Terrier* and *Parish Map*, 1799.
24. F. W. Hackwood, *Wednesbury Workshops* (1889), p. 51.
25. Wednesbury Parish Registers.
26. Ede, *op. cit.*, p. 141-2.
27. Elwell, *op. cit.*, p. 82.
28. As 24 above.
29. Deeds in possession of Edward Elwell Ltd.; Ede, *op. cit.*, p. 234.

30. Plans in Tipton Library.
31. Elwell, *op. cit.*, p. 87.
32. *Robson's London and Birmingham Directory* (1839).
33. Ede, *op. cit.*, p. 235.
34. As 31 above.
35. As 33 above.
36. As 24 above.
37. As 31 above.
38. As 24 above.
39. F. W. Hackwood, *Wednesbury Workshops* (1889), p. 52.
40. Ede, *op. cit.*, p. 286.
41. Elwell, *op. cit.*, p. 88.

XX

HATELEY MILLS
(Manor or Hall Mills)

At the time of Domesday there were no mills in West Bromwich. It is probable that the scanty population of the time used hand mills to grind their corn. By medieval times it was customary for each manor to have established a 'lord's mill', at which all the grain grown within the manor was ground. This obligation, from time to time, provoked opposition, as in the Wednesbury cases in 1316.[1] When the 'lord's mill' was built in the manor of West Bromwich we do not know. We can only guess. It seems probable that there should exist such an establishment by the end of the 13th century, when Richard de Marnham built the manor house (if our estimates for that building are correct). History is completely silent on the story of the mill for more than 300 years. This is not surprising. Such a mill remained the property of the manor and was worked by a miller who was employed for that purpose. It would be unlikely to figure in a rent roll or court roll and in this particular case was never the subject of litigation as in the Wednesbury case cited above.

In the poll tax roll of 1379-80 appear the names of 'Willelm le Melewart' and Margareta, his wife.[2] We cannot be certain that he was the mill-ward of the manorial mill. We do know that when the manorial mill was built, it was sited where one might expect it, on the lowest part of the brook flowing through the 'desmesne' lands (001940). This brook was known as Hobbin's Brook, Hob's Brook, and in recent times the Hobnail Brook. It is probable that the first mill worked from the brook alone, but as the demands on its services increased it was necessary to dam the brook and create a pool or pools.

It is tempting to suggest that, at the end of the 16th century, Walter Stanley, who purchased Bustleholme Mill and is credited with fostering the establishment of the West Bromwich Forge Mill, sought to develop an interest in the new iron industry on his own account by converting the manor mill. Certainly about this time, a windmill was erected nearby, to take care of the corn-grinding side of the business. By 1626 there was a windmill, as well as two watermills, working from a pool on this site.[3] All were included in the 'desmesne lands' and were in hand. This could mean that they were not working, or, more probably, that they were operated by employees of the lord of the manor. They were not out at rent. It is rather curious that four years later, in the rent roll of 1630, the desmesne properties are not itemised, but the collective rent entered alongside a note that they 'are all at lease'. If more was needed to confirm the location of the manorial mill, we find in 1638 the entry that 'the stile at the lower end of the land leading to the lord's mill adjacent to Hockley Heath is in disrepair'.[4] The importance of maintaining the maximum water supply is underlined by the court order in 1686 to 'scour the Hobbin's Brook to the mill pool before Christmas'[5] and at the same court leet that 'no one may prevent water within the Manor flowing towards lord's mills within the same Manor when those mills shall need the water' under penalty of 5s. In 1689 William Turton was ordered to scour the ditch from Hobbin's Brook to the mill pool.[6]

From this time, when the manorial estates of John Shelton were in extreme financial difficulties, the mills were leased to a succession of tenants involved in the iron industry, though in what capacity we cannot be sure. Purchases of rod and bar in the middle of the next century would suggest a forge or rolling-mill, but I cannot find them referred to as such. In 1692 Richard Dickenson leased the mills and mill meadow for 21 years at an annual rent of £12.[7] This lease would normally have expired in 1712-3. The next rent roll names no tenant, but merely informs us that the 'Hall Mills' produced the greatly increased rent of £26.[8] It is highly probable that William Webb had taken over the tenancy from Dickenson, as the 'Survey of Manor Lands, 1720' yields the information that he was the tenant of the mill, mill house and garden, mill meadow, mill pond and part of 'Windmill Leasow'.[9] There was no mention of the windmill. Webb remained the tenant until about 1750. The rent roll for 1731 shows that he had renewed the leases for the mills, one from 1729 for 21 years, and the other from Lady Day 1733 for 18 years. Two separate rents are shown, one for £2 16s. (very small) and the other for £84 15s. (very large). It might be useful if we compare the rents of these mills with the others belonging to the manor.

			Bustleholme	Old Forge	Hall Mills
			£	£	
1626	..	..	20	20	Not stated
1630	..	..	21	20	,, ,,
1649	..	..	10 10s.	7 10s.	,, ,,
1695	..	..	40	20	£12
1719	..	..	Sold in 1709	22	£26
1731	..	..		30	£84 15s. + £2 16s.
1746	..	..		30	£31
1751	..	..		30	£20 + £13
1761	..	..		30	£51 + £13

The smaller amounts for 1649 are probably accounted for by the fact that the roll was for rents payable on 'the Feast of Michael the Archangel' (end of September) and not on Lady Day (25 March) as usual; in other words it was a half year's rent. The amount shown for the Hall mills for 1731 is inexplicable. The outstanding feature of the above table is the rapid growth of the value of the Hall mills and the way it exceeds the value of the Old Forge. We are not to know to what extent these rents are a reflection of the output.

From mid-century the mills parted company. In 1751, Bayley Brett, a well-known factor of nail rod and nails in West Bromwich, and resident in Hateley Heath, took a 21-year lease on the smaller mill at an annual rent of £13, while in 1752, the larger mill was leased for a similar period by Harvey Walklate, at £20 per annum. Within a short time, William Elwell took over the Walklate lease for the same period and rent.[10] Hackwood states that 'in the middle of the last [18th] century there was said to have been an edge-tool forge called Heller's Mill at Hateley Heath'.[11] I can find no other trace of this name and conclude that it was a reference to the Elwell firm. The Walklate tenure must have been of very short duration. Webbs (by that time Thomas Webb) were purchasing bar from the Stour valley forges up to 1748[12] and William Elwell appears for the first time in that field in 1751. Bayley Brett and Co. made their first purchases from that source in 1751-2. From the following year until 1770, the last year for which the detailed sales accounts of Knight's survived, the name changed to William Brett and Co. of Hateley Heath. The change is not made in the rent roll of 1761 where it still appears as Bayley Brett. In 1783 it is William Brett who is listed as a 'nail manufacturer'.[13]

To revert to the larger premises, though 'William Elwell' held it from about 1750 to the early 1830s, they had ceased to purchase bar iron from Knight's by 1753-4. This possibly marked the change in the use of the site. A deed of 1789 enumerating the manorial property refers to an iron foundry, as well as the forge and windmill.[14] Yates's map of 1798 shows the position of one water mill, the windmill and the pools in tandem, but omits any name or description, while an inset on the West Bromwich Enclosure map of 1802-4 shows the 'site plan' of the 'Foundry' but does not include the pools.

In the directory of 1818[15] and 1823[16] the name of James Swindell, iron founder, had replaced that of Brett. This name was in turn superceded by Thomas Dawes of Hateley Heath,[17] who by 1841[18] had expanded to take in the Crookhay Foundry, a quarter of a mile to the west. It still remained 'Thomas Dawes, Ironfounder, Crookhay and Hateley Heath' until 1851,[19] but soon afterwards came a change of ownership and the cessation of interest in the Hateley Heath site.

The firm of William Elwell, which, as we have noted, had occupied the larger mill from about 1750 and had erected the first foundry there, remained until 1823. Hackwood quoting Reeves, states 1836,[20] but it must have moved to Great Bridge a little earlier than that, for the 1835 directory[21] includes the entry 'Ed. Reddell, Iron-founder, Hateley Heath'. The change had already taken place. 'Edward J. Reddell' ceased to operate there between 1842 and 1845, probably absorbed by Thomas Dawes who continued for another 15 years. The 1834 1in. O.S. map marks the pools and buildings, but no windmill, and the 1849 6ch. to 1in. map[22] shows in detail the two pools, lade and buildings, but no wording.

There can be little doubt that the sinking of the Millpool Colliery about 1839 affected the water supply and later, Millfield Colliery was sunk on the site of the old foundry.

Housing to the north side of the tall flats in Rydding Lane occupied the site in 1969. The mound of the one-time windmill may still be seen, but the last of the pools is now being infilled with refuse and 'Hobbin's Brook' flows underground through a conduit.

NOTES

1. *Plea Rolls,* 1316 (*S.H.C.,* vol. XII, pp. 104-5).
2. *Poll Tax Roll,* 1379-80 (*S.H.C.,* vol. XVII, p. 170).
3. West Bromwich Manorial Rent Roll, 1626.
4. West Bromwich Manorial Court Roll, 1638.
5. *Ibid.,* 1686.
6. *Ibid.,* 1689.
7. West Bromwich Manorial Rent Roll, 1692.
8. *Ibid.,* 1719.
9. P.R.O., C 103/129.
10. West Bromwich Manorial Rent Roll, 1746, annotations.

11.   F. W. Hackwood, *Wednesbury Workshops* (1889), p. 50.
12.   Knight's Account Books.
13.   *Bailey's Western and Midland Directory* (1783).
14.   Indenture of Bargain and Sale (18 May 1789), enrolled in Common Pleas, Easter Term, 29 Geo. III, roll 142. Abstract of Deeds, Miscellaneous Documents, West Bromwich Reference Library.
15.   *Parson and Bradshaw Directory* (1818).
16.   *Wrightson's Triennial Directory of Birmingham* (1823).
17.   *White's Staffordshire Directory* (1834).
18.   *Pigot's National and Commercial Directory* (1841).
19.   *White's History and Directory of Staffordshire* (1851).
20.   F. W. Hackwood, *Wednesbury Workshops* (1889), p. 28.
21.   *Pigot's National and Commercial Directory* (1835).
22.   Joseph Cooksey (?), *A Map of West Bromwich* (1849); 6ch. to 1in.

XXI

BILSTON MILL

The Bilston mill stood on the insignificant Bilston brook, about half a mile to the south-south-west of the parish church of Bilston (951961). This is another water mill which is unsatisfactory to the historian in that there is little in the way of documentary records. An added difficulty is that a corn-grinding windmill existed at Bilston, a little to the north-east of the church in the Mountpleasant area, from at least the early 15th century until the present, though not continuously, and rarely does a reference make clear a distinction. It may be that the existence of such a windmill is an indication of the inadequacy of the available water power to grind the corn for what was no more than a large village. The population of Bilston did not reach 3,000 until early in the 19th century.

The Rev. Richard Ames tells us that he had had the opportunity of reading a number of documents belonging to the Robbins family.[1] Among these was one, a copy of Surrender, dated 1378, by which Thomas Robbins and his wife Juliana 'do give to Sir William Poort, ye priest of Bilston, and John Robbins one messuage, one water-mill etc.'. For 'an Harriott' was given one cow valued 6s. 8d. and for admittance, 8s.

He tells of another document, c. 1383, which informs us that Robert Rowley, late of Bilston (miller), did in his lifetime surrender to James Perry and Thomas Smith those two dwellings etc.

Another deed of 1553 stated that Roger de Boverucks sold one half of a mill in Bilston to Adam Bate.

The parish registers provide us with the names of early 18th-century millers but make no distinction between the two mills. Henry Downing was miller in 1716 and 1717, and John Smith in 1720. John Stokes who was miller in 1722, was referred to as miller and wood-screw maker in 1726. By 1730 it would appear that he had ceased the occupation of miller and was named as a wood-screw maker only.

William Yates's map of 1775 clearly marks the position of the water mill but omits the windmill. His revised map of 1798 still shows the former but adds a canal arm to collieries in the vicinity, cutting the brook just above the mill. A sketch map of 1781 names it as Bickley's Mill, by which name it had been known for at least 14 years, but gives no hint of its use.[2]

In 1818 Edward Hickman was named as the corn miller at Bilston Mill while Joseph Howell and Joseph Owen followed similar occupations at Mount Pleasant.[3] There were other mills, probably steam, in Mill Street and Church Street by that time.

By 1834,[4] though Joseph Howell was still operating at Mount Pleasant, the 'Bread Company' had taken over at Bilston Mill. A note adds the explanation that 'The South Staffordshire Bread Company established in 1832 have here a large establishment for grinding corn and for making bread on a patent plan'. It is probable that by this time the water mill had ceased to operate. The first edition of the 1in. O.S. map reveals that the line of the stream had been moved somewhat, and that a quarry and factories had covered most of the adjacent site. It is an interesting fact that the windmill is now marked again, apparently rebuilt.

The water is now concealed in a culvert, but the names of Brook Street and Brook Terrace mark its former position.

NOTES

1. *Bilston Parish Registers,* reprint Parish Register Soc., p. 173.
2. Stafford County Record Office; Q/SB A. 1781.
3. *Parson and Bradshaw Directory* (1818).
4. *White's Staffordshire Directory* (1834).

XXII

WILLINGSWORTH MILL

The Parkes family of Wednesbury, who played such an important part in the development of the iron industry in this district in the early 17th century, acquired Willingsworth Hall (976946) in 1598.[1] Though the unimpressive Lea brook flowed close by there is no evidence that the Parkes attempted to harness the stream for any of their undertakings, but rather established their operations along the main waters of the Tame (*see* Wednesbury Mills, Walsall Bloom-smithy, and West Bromwich Old Forge). The Lea brook was, however, diverted to form a small lake or pool on the south side of the Hall. This may not have occurred until the next century.

During the first half of the 18th century a family named Wiggins were operating a number of corn mills in South Staffordshire, both windmills and water mills. These included mills at Sedgley, Darlaston, Wednesbury, and Walsall New Mills. To these must be added a small water corn mill at the south end of Willingsworth pool. We have the record[2] in 1711 of the burial of Henry Wiggins, senior, of Willingsworth Mill.

How long this mill continued we do not know, for though the Yates map of 1775 shows the existence of the pool, there is no mill marked at that time. It is possible that this is a case of omission as a sketch map of 1781 shows a mill and names it as Willingsworth Blade Mill.[3] This was to cease soon afterwards, for in 1783 an Act was promoted to provide for the extension of the Wednesbury Canal from Ryder's Green to the Broadwaters engine and to provide six collateral cuts, yet a rent roll of the Sedgley section of the manor of Dudley,[4] shows that a James Smith was still paying rent for Willingsworth Hall, mill and pool in 1788, lately held by Thomas Tibbitts. The new canal was to pass through the Willingsworth site and two of the cuts were to originate from Willingsworth pool. The immediate vicinity was to become the site for the Willingsworth furnaces and ironworks which were to dominate the locality until the Second World War.[5] It is appropriate that the bridge over the canal should still bear the name 'Wiggin's Mill Bridge'.

NOTES

1. Ede, *op. cit.*, p. 126.
2. Wednesbury Parish Register.
3. Stafford County Record Office; Q/SB A.1781.
4. William Salt Library, Stafford; 21/39.
5. Ede, *op. cit.*, p. 271.

XXIII

THE TIPTON MILLS ON THE TAME

The stretch of the Tame from Great Bridge to Wednesbury Bridge has a confused history, being something of an industrial palimpsest. It is highly probable that water mills existed here for centuries, but little of their story can be traced.

Part of this area is known as Toll End, the derivation of which name has given rise to speculation. The locality name would appear to have been a family name at one time, a not unusual occurrence. The Scottish subsidy roll of 1327 names Joh'e atte Telle.[1] In the next century, 1460, we find a conveyance from John Tolle and John Packet to Thomas Gardynere, a chaplain, with reversion to the descendants of John Packet, of a mill and some 77 acres in Tybynton.[2]

From time to time there are references to a mill in Tipton, such as that in 1349,[3] but with no hint as to site. Richard Tole and Margery, his wife, conveyed to Thomas and Richard Parkes a water mill and other property in Tipton in 1597.[4] The Parkes, father and son, were among the foremost ironmongers of the region at that time.

In October 1654 John Wheeler prepared 'A inventarie of all thinges belong and being at Tole End Mills ffor Mr Richard Foley the elder'.[5] The mills consisted of a water mill, disused, a windmill, and living accommodation. Since the relevant accounts for these mills have not been found, evidence of the conversion of these corn mills to a forge is lacking. However an item 'to Richard Wheeler ye Acc. of building Tipton Mills, £152 10s.' occurs in 1671.[6]

A map of the intended Birmingham Navigation, 1767,[7] shows but one mill, with a pool, Tipton Forge, on this reach. Yates's map of 1775 shows the same forge as the sole water mill in a position 976934. A sketch map of 1781 still marks it as the only mill, but supplies the information, 'Tipton Forge and Slitting Mill'.[8]

On this site, or very close to it, there was later 'Moore's Mill', belonging to Daniel Moore, 'formerly Price Thomas's forge'.[9] It is probable that this is a reference to Thomas Price, ironmaster of Tipton. When Shaw wrote this in 1798, he described the edifice as being 'one slitting mill worked by water with two undershot wheels, to which is now added a steam engine and one of the water wheels is a substitute for a fly-wheel and does very well'. Although Daniel Moore, of Tipton, ironmaster, died about 1802-3,[10] the forge was still named 'Moore's Mill' on the Earl of Dudley's Mines map of 1812, and at that date it was still the only mill marked. Parkes[11] states that a water mill was still in use in 1820 at 'Taylor's Foundry' in Toll End. The mill dam was still shown on Fowler's map of Tipton, 1849, when the factory was named Toll End Ironworks. The whole of the site was to become later part of the Toll End sewage works, but the name is perpetuated in 'Moore's Mill Lane'.

A few hundred yards downstream from Tipton Forge *alias* Moore's Mill *alias* Toll End Mill was Gold's Mill (or Bagnall's Mill) which was to become the site of Bagnall's Gold's Hill Ironworks. The first definite reference to the use of this site is the Dawson 2in. map of 1816, when it is shown as Gold's Mill. It then worked direct from the stream and possessed no pool. The number and size of the buildings had grown considerably when it was marked on the 1834 first edition 1in. O.S. map. We are told by Reeves, writing in 1836, that the 'Gold's Hill ironworks was originally a slitting-mill, worked by a water wheel as were all the original ironworks. Mr. Saunders converted it into a forge. Mr. Aston succeeded Saunders, and Mr. J. Bagnall and Sons succeeded Aston. It is now the property of Mrs. Hill'.[12] It is unfortunate that Reeves did not quote dates or supply other details. It has not been possible to trace Mr. Saunders, though there is evidence that Astons possessed an ironworks in the Ocker Hill locality. Apart from this mention, we have no reference at all to Mrs. Hill and it is difficult to accept this as fact if we trace the history of J. Bagnall and Sons through Hackwood.[13] Hackwood tells us, again without dates, that John Bagnall, from being a ground bailiff in Tipton at the end of the 18th century, became a coalmaster on the purchase of mines in the Toll End, Coppice and Lea Bank areas. He then entered the iron business by the purchase of a furnace, built by Michael Tony in 1803, and took his sons into partnership as John Bagnall and Sons. Next he built the Gold's Green furnaces and followed that by the purchase of the Toll End Iron Works from the Birmingham Coal Co. Later he acquired the Lea Brook Iron Works from Messrs. Bates and Robins, for whom John Hartland undertook the management. It is difficult to put precise dates on these changes. The firm is not mentioned in the 1818 *History and Directory of Staffordshire,* but the 1823 *Triennial Directory of Birmingham* includes 'John Bagnall and Sons of Golds Green'. From that time onwards the name appears regularly until the 1876 *Post Office Directory,* though by that time the firm no longer existed. The partnership had been dissolved in 1856 and when William, son of John Bagnall, died in 1863, his brother James remained as sole proprietor. When he died in 1872, he bequeathed the concern to his brother Richard, who declined the management. A limited company was formed, but it was soon faced with bankruptcy. It is unlikely that the old water mill played any part in the Gold's Hill Iron Works, which were built around it, downstream from the Toll End works. A daughter of John Bagnall, step-sister of William, James and Richard, married a Thomas Davis of Gold's Hill. On the site of the old Gold's Mill, a corn mill was erected and the firm of Davis and Bagnall, corn millers, of Gold's Hill Mill, appeared regularly from the 1834 *White's Directory* until the 1856 *Post Office Directory*. The mill appears to have existed after this date for an undated sketch map prepared for the Bagnall Sales,[14] shows the 'Corn Mill', in the angle between the Tame Valley canal and the Danks Branch canal. It is not possible to say whether it was still water-powered. The whole area now forms part of the electricity generating station.

Whether the Lea brook (979945) site was ever used by a water-powered mill is open to doubt. No indication of such a possibility is to be found before 1834 when, on the first edition 1in. O.S. map, the name Leabrook Mill occurs. This was to be the site of the Lea Brook Iron works, which was, we are told, the last acquisition of the Bagnall firm.[15] Certainly the name of the mill had been removed from the third reprint of the above map, *c.* 1860. The ironworks was not to suffer the fate of the Gold's Hill works for it was rescued by the family and was managed by W. G. Bagnall as the Lea Brook and Imperial Iron-works and was still in operation at the end of the century.

NOTES

1. *Scottish Subsidy Roll, 1327* (*S.H.C.*, vol. VII, p. 234).
2. *Final Concord, 1460* (*S.H.C.*, vol. XI. p. 238).
3. *Plea Rolls, 1349* (*S.H.C.*, vol. XII, pp. 92-3).
4. *Final Concord, 1596* (*S.H.C.*, vol. XVI, p. 173).
5. Hereford County Record Office, K.A., folio 5.
6. Hereford County Record Office; F/VI/KBF/32. In subsequent years there are accounts for their repair.
7. R. Whitworth, *Plan of Intended Navigation from Birmingham* (1767); William Salt Library, Stafford.
8. Stafford County Record Office; Q/SB A.1781.
9. Stebbing Shaw, *op. cit.*, p. 136.
10. F. W. Hackwood, *History of Tipton* (1891), p. 24.
11. J. Parkes, *History of Tipton* (1915), p. 27.
12. Jos. Reeves, *op. cit.*, p. 113.
13. F. W. Hackwood, *History of Tipton* (1891), pp. 44 *et. seq.*
14. Sales Sketch map of Bagnall property, undated; Tipton Central Library.
15. As 13 above.

XXIV

PARKES'S HALL MILL

Parkes's (formerly Persehouse's) Hall Mill (933928) was part of the property of the manor of Sedgley and as such of Lord Dudley.

A survey of the manor in 1614 states that 'Edward Persehouse of Persehouse's Hall holds to him and his heirs of the aforesaid Earl as of his Manor of Sedgley aforesaid by copy of Court Roll according to the custom of the said Manor, one tenement in Woodsetton viz one messuage in which he dwells called Persehouses Hall with, inter alia, one close called Mill Leasow with a Mill built thereupon and one close called Mylners'.[1] For all of which, and other properties, he was to pay suit of court every three weeks, suit at the two Great Courts, fealty, herriott when due, serve as 'biddle' and pay an annual rent of £1 10s. 7½d.

It seems that this property was to remain a copyhold tenancy for nearly 200 years.

In 1789 Hannah Sharp surrendered to Thomas Dowler, Brassfounder and Candle Stick Maker, of Birmingham, 'the Mill Meadow and all that one Water Corn Mill situate in Woodsetton, formerly part of a certain tenement called Persehouse Hall'.[2] At the next court leet there was a confirmation to Dowler in more elaborate terms giving greater details of property and position.

It seems that Hannah Sharp and Dowler were sub-tenants, for even after more than 170 years the Persehouse family were still tenants-in-chief.

In August, 1792,[3] William Parkes *alias* Persehouse, infant, only son of Henry Parkes *alias* Persehouse, late of Wolverhampton, malster, deceased, was admitted as tenant of the manor in respect of the Mill Leasow, Mill

Meadow, Little Meadow, water corn mill etc. in Woodset-ton, formerly part of a certain tenement called Persehouse Hall, and now in the possession of Isaac Smith. For this he paid a fine of admission of 18s. 11d. and agreed to pay a chief rent of 18s. 11d. and herriott as necessary. It will be noticed that the extent of the property had shrunk. It is not clear whether he continued to hold it and sublet it or whether he surrendered the holding almost immediately.

In December of the same year 1792, the same property was conveyed by the lord of the manor to John Beebee and Edward Simpson in equal undivided moieties.[4]

John Beebee and partners held the property, still as a water corn mill, with Isaac Smith as occupant, until 1798 when they surrendered it to Lord Dudley, as lord of the manor.[5] John James became the next tenant, holding it for six years. At the Court Baron of April 1804, the executors of John James, deceased, prayed admittance as tenants, surrendered the tenancy to the lord of the manor who in turn surrendered it to William Gardner of Kingswinford. This would seem an unnecessarily long way of conveying the lease but no doubt someone benefited. Throughout the time Isaac Smith remained as occupant of the mill itself, probably as the miller.

After something like 200 known years as a water corn mill, its existence was to come to an end. The 1834 1in. O.S. map shows an enlarged pool. The tithe award of 1843 shows that the pool had become a reservoir, which by means of a pump in an adjacent pumphouse, supplied part of the town of Dudley with water.

The reservoir still existed in 1971.

NOTES

1. *Survey of the Manor of Sedgley (1614)*; Dudley Central Library, L.D., Box 7/9.
2. Sedgley Manorial Court Roll, 1789.
3. *Ibid.*, August 1792.
4. *Ibid.*, December 1792.
5. *Ibid.*, 1798.

LORD DUDLEY'S (COSELEY) BLADE MILL

This small mill lay within the manor of Sedgley and as part of the manor was the property of the Earls of Dudley. It lay close to the left or north bank of the small stream which flowed from Sedgley to Tipton Green, near to the Tipton border (946928).

John Beebee became the tenant of the blade-mill, from Lord Dudley in 1792,[1] the same year in which he took over the tenancy of the Parkes's Hall mill.

A map of 1798 shows the mill and several adjoining fields as being copyhold of John Beebee.[2]

A later map of 1810 names it as Lord Dudley's Coseley Blade Mill, but does not state the tenant, though it gives the occupant as Jeremiah Whitehouse.[3]

Considerable mining and canal construction in the area may have been responsible for the disappearance of this establishment shortly afterwards. There is no indication of it by 1834.[4]

The tithe map of 1843 on a large scale (6ch. to 1in.) shows no sign of pool or race which had been a feature of the earlier maps. An interesting point however is that the accompanying schedule shows that some buildings on the site were occupied by Benjamin Whitehouse.

NOTES

1. Stafford County Record Office; C 107/74.
2. Dudley Reference Library; L.D. 884C.
3. Dudley Reference Library; L.D. 847C.
4. 1in. O.S. map, 1st edition.

TIPTON BLOOMFIELD MILL

One of the small tributaries of the Upper Tame rose in the vicinity of Sedgley, flowing in a south-easterly direction through Bloomfield, crossing the present Church Lane, skirting the north side of the present cemetery to join the Tame at the site of the sewage works in Toll End. Today, largely due to canal construction, little trace of this stream is to be seen, yet in former days, small though it was, it provided the power for a series of water mills. Of these we should note the one at Bloomfield (949930) where the stream crossed the Dudley-Tipton boundary.

This must have been one of the earliest ironworking mills in the district. We have no record of it working as a corn mill, though it is always possible that it was so engaged before the end of the 13th century. An inquisition post mortem held in 1279 on the property of the late William fitz Geoffrey de Tybyngton, described him as the uncle of Henry de Heronville and brother of Isabella, wife of Robert de Blomere.[1] In the following year his widow, described as Alice, widow of William fitz Geoffrey fitz Warine, brought suit for dower against her nephew Henry de Heronville and brother-in-law, Robert de Blome.[2] There was a similar case in 1302 when Christina, widow of John, son of Walter de Mere, of Dudley, brought suit for dower against Robert de Blomer claiming one third part of the water mill, four acres of land and four acres of meadow in Tipton.[3] The importance of this case to us is that it points to the fact that at that time the water mill was held by a bloomer; in other words it was already a bloom-smithy.

It appears that Robert the 'bloomer' was operating the mill for over 20 years. That the craft of a bloom-smith continued after the days of Robert, is shown by an assize held in 1331, to enquire if Roger le Blomere of Tybynton and Robert de Heghhegge had unjustly desseised Amice the Deye of 20 acres of land and two acres of pasture in Tybynton.[4]

Our next references to this establishment are taken from the parish registers of Tipton, more than 300 years later, when it is named as the 'bloomsmithy'. In 1650 and 1652 we find the baptisms of the children of Richard Whitehouse of the 'Blom Smithe' and Diane, his wife. From 1676 to 1694 there are a series of entries relating to the Parkes family of the 'Bloom Smithy'. The dates are worth noting, as they are par-ticularly late for this type of work. The Walsall bloom-smithy (*q.v.*) had ceased to function by about 1617 and the Friar Park bloom-smithy (*q.v.*) by 1592. We are tempted to question whether the Tipton bloom-smithy was still operating as such in 1694 or whether the name persisted while the smithy had become a 'bloomery and chafery' as in the case of most forges.

One branch of the Dudley family was long resident in Tipton, many of them being associated with the iron trade in one way or another. The celebrated Dud Dudley spent at least his early days here but it is not possible to associate him with the Bloomfield smithy. Some 50 years earlier, in 1553, John Dudley, Duke of Northum-berland, had bought property very shortly before he was attainted for high treason and executed. The name of bloom-smithy was to linger on for another century yet. In 1761 Thomas Fieldhouse in a survey referred to it as the Bloomsmithy Mill Estate,[5] while in 1774 the same gentleman produced a delightful hand-coloured plan on parchment of the estates of the Dudley family in Tipton, including the Bloomsmith Mill Estate.[6] The mill-pool, the recently constructed Brindley Canal and Hurst Lane are shown. The original survey map shows the same fields with the addition of areas but the omission of the mill buildings.[7] The line of the canal has been added later.

Yates's map of 1775 shows the mill-pool but no indication of a water-mill, though this does not necessarily mean that it had ceased to exist. A jury stated that 'We present James Maullin of the Village of Cosley within this Manor for stopping and turning a Water Course in a certain Lane called Wallbrook Lane, leading to the Bloomsmithy Mill, whereby the Water is hindered from having its due course and renders the said Lane impassable. And we order and agree that the said James Maullin do open the said Watercourse on or before the second day of December next on pain of forfeiting to the Lord of the Manor, One pound Nineteen shilling and eleven pence on his neglect'.[8]

About 1780 James Keir of West Bromwich set up a chemical factory on this site to produce alkali, soap, white and red lead.[9] We are told that it was established there to take advantage of the 'cheapness of fuel and convenience of canal' and that it 'occupies a space of several acres adjoining the Birmingham Canal, receiving the power required for its various operations from two water-wheels and two fire engines'. By the end of the century the manufacture of soap had expanded to such an extent as to consume almost the whole of the output of the alkali produced. The lead compounds found a market in the glass industry of Stourbridge and as glazes at Wedgwood's pottery at Etruria. Joshia Wedgwood was customer, fellow member of the Lunar Society of Birmingham and a personal friend of James Keir. Before 1814.[10] Keir had retired from the business which was carried on by Alexander Blair, a former partner. The soap factory continued until 1842.

By 1795 the remainder of the Bloomfield Estate, including the 99-year lease of the colliery and farmhouse, was advertised for sale.[11] The Bloomfield Ironworks was erected here in 1826.[12]

The first edition of the 1in. O.S. map still showed the mill-pool and named the Bloomfield Forge in the

A Survey of the *Bloomsmithy Mill Estate* lying in the Parish of Tipton, in the County of Stafford the Late **Thos. Dudley's Gent.**

A
a . r . p
7 . 1 . 16

B
a . r . p
4 . 0 . 8

D

C

THE CANAL

a . r . p
6 . 0 . 1

a . r . p
2 . 2 . 30

E
a . r . p
4 . 1 . 31

F
a . r . p
3 . 2 . 0

H a . r . p
1 . 0 . 2

G
a . r . p
1 . 2 . 0

L
a . r . p
1 . 0 . 2

K
a . r . p
1 . 3 . 0

HURST LANE

Scale of Chains and Links

	References	A	
A	Great Moor	7 .	1
B	Engine Leaſow	4 .	0
C	The Rough	2 .	2
D	The Mowing Meadow	6 .	0
E	The far Meadow	4 .	1
F	The far Pool Tail Piece	3 .	2
G	The nether Pool Tail Piece & far Pool	1 .	2
H	The Pool Piece	1 .	0
I	The Mill Pool		1
K	The Piece acroſs the Lane	1 .	3
L	The House Gardens Barns foldyard Mill &c	1 .	0
	Total	33 .	3

Survey'd in the Year 1761 by Tho. Fieldhouse
& this Copied by Thos. Dudley in 1774.

Plan 4: Plan of Tipton Bloomsmithy Mill, 1761.

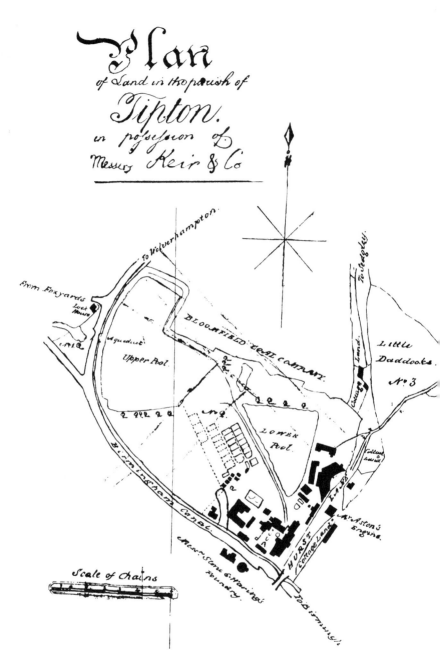

Plan 5: Plan of Keir's factory, Tipton, *c.* 1790.

area as did the Fowler map of Tipton in 1849, but the later reprint of the 1in. O.S. in the later 1850s showed that the Birmingham to Wolverhampton line of the Stour Valley Railway and the Dudley to Wolverhampton line had intersected on the site and had obliterated the old mill-pool.

NOTES

1. *Inq. P.M.*, 1279 (*S.H.C.*, vol. VI, p. 142).
2. *Plea Rolls*, 1280 (*S.H.C.*, vol. VI, p. 99).
3. *Plea Rolls*, 1302 (*S.H.C.*, vol. VII, p. 97).
4. *Plea Rolls*, 1331 (*S.H.C.*, vol. XI, p. 21).
5. J. Parkes, *op. cit.*, p. 27.
6. T. Fieldhouse, *Survey of the Bloomsmithy Mill Estate* (1761); Tipton Central Library.
7. Wodehouse Wombourne Collection.
8. Sedgley Manorial Court Roll, 1779.
9. Stebbing Shaw, *op. cit.*, p. 136.
10. Tipton Rate Books.
11. Aris's *Birmingham Gazette*, 27 April 1795.
12. F. W. Hackwood, *History of Tipton* (1891), p. 43.

XXVII

PARTRIDGE'S (HORSELEY) MILL

This mill situated a short distance to the east of Church Lane, Tipton (965932), seems to have been the principal corn mill in that town for much of the 18th century.

Much of the history of this mill may be gathered from the abstract of deeds of an estate, drawn in 1795, when part of that estate, 'The Coppice', was chosen as the site of Tipton New Church.[1] The estate was sold by Philip Foley to Joan Nightingale, spinster, of Robaston in the county of Stafford, in 1708. This raises the question as to whether the mill had played any part in the Foley iron operations prior to that date. If it did, it was probably the one which appears in Philip Foley's Account Books as Tyb Green (or Tib Green or Tipgreen) Forge.[2] This operated as part of the Staffordshire complex from 1702 to 1709. Obadiah Lane was the manager until 1707 when he was replaced by John Wheeler. 'Brookshaw the ffiner at Typgreen' lived in a house on the premises. The forge was sold and delivered to Thomas Hart at midsummer 1709.

After passing through various hands the estate became the possession of the Eginton family. A conveyance of 1742 of the estate from John and Lucy Eginton to Jeremiah Eginton specifically mentions one water corn mill and one windmill.[3]

An indenture of 1768 stated that the mill was lately in the occupation of John Partridge and James Jones.[4]

Yates's map of 1775, marks a water mill and pool on this stretch of the stream but seems to place it a little lower than the site we have given above.

A sketch map of 1781 names the mill as Partridge's Corn Mill.[5] This is no proof of course that Partridge still occupied it at that date. A map of the Toll End Canal and the mining property of Messrs. Dixon, Amphlett and Bedford, made from a survey of 1785 shows it as Finch's Mill and Pool (formerly Partridge's). Seven years later, in 1792, a map was made of the Horseley Estate of Messrs. Dixon, Amphlett, Bedford and Co., fails to name the property other than as 'The Blade Mill'. An annotation to this map states that it was purchased from Finch's devisees. Presumably it was converted to a blade-mill by Finch.

It is interesting to see that the Earl of Dudley's mines map of 1812, 20 years later, still names it as Partridge's Mill Pool, especially as it also shows that the Horseley Furnaces and Ironworks had replaced the blade-mill.

It is difficult, if not impossible, to identify the pool on the first edition 1in. O.S. map of 1834, though it must still have been in existence.

The 1822 estate map of the Dixon, Amphlett and Bedford properties, and Fowler's Plan of the Parish of Tipton, 1849, both show the pool and canals with the adjacent Horseley Ironworks. When in 1857, at the sale of this company's property a plan of the Horseley Estate was prepared, it showed an almost identical layout.

We are told that 'A water-wheel originally provided power to drive the machinery at the old Horseley works, then at the rear of Tipton cemetery and up to the time of the demolition of these works, if, by any means, the steam engine was put out of action, the old water-wheel was set in motion'.[6] It would appear that the steam-engine was installed about 1804 for in the parish books for 1805 occurs for the first time, the entry 'Elijah Southall, paid for "Stem" mill, 16s. 3d.'. This is a reference to the Poor Rate. The old works were demolished about 1867 and the later works bearing the same name were constructed south of the canal.

NOTES

1. J. Parkes, *op. cit.*, pp. 76 *et seq.*
2. Hereford County Record Office; F/VI/GAF/24-29.
3. *Final Concord*, 1742.
4. As 1 above.
5. Stafford County Record Office; Q/SB A.1781.
6. J. Parkes, *op. cit.*, p. 26.

XXVIII

DUDLEY: PRIORY AND CASTLE (SHIRT'S) MILLS

The *Victoria County History* states 'no mill was held
by the Lords of Dudley. The Priors seem to have
possessed one but there is no mention of it until after
the Dissolution (1538)'.[1] These statements do not agree
with the facts as we find them. This may be due to
the fact that Dudley Castle and the adjacent land was
within the manor of Sedgley rather than in that of
Dudley in medieval times. Both manors were the property
of the Lords of Dudley.

A small stream, a tributary of the Tame, rose in
Dudley close to the site of the present Town Hall.
A very insignificant brook, it flowed northward through
the site of the Priory grounds, to the west of Castle Hill,
until it reached the northern end of that ridge. It then
turned and flowed in an east-north-easterly direction
through Tipton. It provided the power to operate two
water mills, Priory (943909) and Castle (945918) mills,
before it crossed the Tipton boundary. In both cases
the stream was dammed to form a small mill-pool.

A survey of the manor of Dudley of 1272 contains
no mention of a mill[2] but the survey of the manor of
Sedgley states that 'there are two water-mills worth
yearly 53s. 4d. . . . also the mill of Penyval [on the
west of the watershed] is worth yearly 13s. 4d.'.[3] The
surveys also contain the value of the services to be
rendered in the manor. William the Miller was detailed
to mow corn, mow, make and carry hay, and gather nuts,
and 'his service is worth 18½d.'; also 'Richard the miller
ought to bring up a whelp for ½ year and its keep is
worth 6d. yearly'.

Shortly afterwards in 1274-5, we have the case of the murder of 'Thomas, the Miller' at Horsepool.[4] Horsepool was adjacent to the junction of the present Priory and Stone Streets.

Another survey of the manor of Sedgley, 1292, includes Dudley Castle, two water mills worth yearly 29s. 4d. and a fish pond and fishery worth 13s. 4d.[5] Presumably one of these mills was the Castle Mill in the Old Park, but it is not certain that the Priory Mill was included in the property of the lord at this time.

In 1322, John de Somery, Lord of Dudley, died seised of two water mills in Dudley.[6] This again raises the question as to whether at that time there was another mill on the stream or whether the Priory Mill was the property of the lord. We do know that the Priory, so close to the castle walls, was endowed by the Lords of Dudley, was always greatly under the influence of them and that after the Dissolution the grounds and buildings reverted to them. A contemporary dower suit of 1322 does nothing to clarify the matter. In this Richard de Thorp and Margaret, his wife, sued William de Bereford for one-third of, *inter alia,* two water mills and one weaving-mill (?) in Himley, Swinford, Sedgley and Dudley.[7]

Five years later, 1327, the Scottish subsidy roll for Dudley, contains the name of another Thomas 'le Muleward'.[8]

Despite the importance of these mills as a source of manorial revenue in the Middle Ages, it was not unknown for one to be leased for an annual rental. The case of the Wednesbury Mill and the Hillary family has already been quoted. In 1437 William Freebody died, seised of a water mill in Dudley.[9] He held it jointly with Margaret, his wife, of Sir John Sutton, kt., Lord of Dudley. Maybe this was the same William Freebody who was the lord of the manor of West Bromwich at that time, though the name of Freebody was common in Dudley.

The *Victoria County History* suggests that the Priors held one of the mills up to the Dissolution of 1538. In 1610-11 there was reference to a windmill in Dudley, lately of the Priory, but 'now in the possession of Lord Dudley'.[10] This may well have been the windmill which stood near to the present Stafford Street, on the top of the hill.

A rate assessment for the year 1649 names Robert Dudley, gent., as paying 3s. 4d. for Saltwater Mill and other property. It is not clear that this was one of these two mills or whether it was on the other side of the watershed at Saltwells, between Netherton and Brierley Hill.[11]

In 1741, we find that there was a 'water corn-mill annexed to the site of the priory'.[12]

The tithe map of 1787 marks the positions of both Priory and Castle Mill pools.[13] They are shown as the property of the Lord Dudley.

William Yates, on his map of 1775, marks both these sites as possessing water mills but they must have ceased to operate as such soon after. The Dudley Canal Company was formed in 1776 and the Dudley Tunnel, taking the canal under the town was opened in 1792. This canal took the water from this stream to supply its top level. The quarrying of the Castle Mill basin removed part of the mill site but the name persisted.

Jer. Mathews's map of Dudley Canal Navigations, 1825, names the castle Mill but shows no pool, only the basin.[14] It does show a pool or lake in the Priory grounds which are stated to be the property of the Rt. Hon. the Lord Dudley and Ward.

A plan dated 1803 is headed 'Plan of the Canal Branch from the Birmingham Canal to the Lime Works at Shirt's Mill, Dudley'.[15] This appears to be a renaming of the Castle Mill. The plan does not actually show the mill nor give any clue to the work carried on there, though we may assume that it was no longer a water mill. The name 'Shirt's Mill' is used on the first edition 1in. O.S. map.

By 1835, according to J. Treasure's map of Dudley the name had reverted to Castle Mill. By this time no water was indicated at the Priory site.[16]

In 1841, David Addenbrook of Gornal Wood was engaged to take charge of all boats of customers of Trustees, brought on the Birmingham Canal to Castle Mill to load limestone or coal. He was paid £4 12s. per month.[17]

The British Welding and Machine Co., Ltd., was formed in 1929 on the Earl of Dudley's 'Castle Mill Site' formerly the Earl's locomotive works.[18]

We have found no evidence that these two water mills were ever used for any other purpose than that of grinding corn.

NOTES

1.   *V.C.H., Worcs.,* vol. 3 (1945), p. 102.
2.   *Survey of the Manor of Dudley,* 1272 (*S.H.C.,* vol. IX, pt. 2, p. 25.
3.   *Survey of the Manor of Sedgley,* 1272 (*S.H.C.,* vol. IX, pt. 2, p. 28.
4.   *Assize Roll,* 3/4 Edw. I, 1026m 38.
5.   *Survey of the Manor of Sedgley,* 1272 (*S.H.C.,* vol. IX, pt. 2, p. 32.
6.   *Inq. P.M.,* 1322 (*S.H.C.,* 1911, p. 353).
7.   *Plea Roll,* 1322 (*S.H.C.,* vol. IX, pt. 1, p. 85).
8.   *Scottish Subsidy Roll,* 1327 (*S.H.C.,* vol. VII, pt. 1, p. 229).
9.   *Inq. P.M.,* 1437; Dudley Library, No. 46.
10. pat. 8 Jas. I, pt. XLII.
11. Dudley Archives, 19/36.
12. Recovery, R. East; 14 Geo. II, rot. 199.
13. Court Book, No. 24; Dudley Reference Library.
14. Dudley Library; 1556 C.
15. *Ibid.,* 1704 C.
16. *Ibid.,* not numbered.
17. *Ibid.,* Local File 'c', No. 57.
18. *Ibid.,* General Notes, No. 31, p. 78.

XXIX

FISHER'S MILL

Fisher's Mill (977926) was one of the less significant of the Tame Valley mills.

James Fisher, a Tipton industrialist at the end of the 18th century, was a staunch supporter of Tipton Church, which was being rebuilt on the new site at that time. His name occurs on the list of Trustees responsible for the Tipton Church Act of 1794.[1] An inscription on the treble bell of the parish church reads 'The gift of James Fisher, Ironmaster. Thomas Meares of London fecit 1798'. He became churchwarden in 1799.

Though he was obviously a man of some affluence, we cannot be sure where he carried on his business of iron-master. It is possible that he was the operator of the Sheepwash Mill at this time for he was the owner or lessee of much of the land bounded by the river, Sheepwash Lane, Whitehall Road and the Turnpike Road near to the Great Bridge toll gate. Though deeds for this land exist from 1713[2] there was not any suggestion of a possible water mill until 1775, when there was stated to be 'one acre of land covered with water'. James Fisher purchased the property in 1798. He was soon in financial difficulties for in 1801 he mortgaged to William Brueton of Bilston for £1,000 at five per cent. a considerable amount of property 'and also all that forge mill and steam engine and all that other erections and buildings with appurtenances erected, built and set up on the same by the said James Fisher'. This suggests a water mill aided by steam. Fisher never redeemed the mortgage and in 1811, increased his indebtedness by borrowing £2,000 from Elizabeth, widow of William Brueton. In 1816, Fisher and his partners became bankrupt, legal disputes between rival creditors continuing for two or three years. In 1816 the property was still stated to include a 'Forge Mill and Steam Engine'. An undated estate plan of the Fisher estates shows that he occupied a large house, outbuildings and gardens facing into Whitehall Road.[3] In 1801, he received seven small parcels of land which served to consolidate this previous holding.[4] At this date there was no indication of the existence of 'Fisher Mill'.

The first and indeed the only map showing this mill is the 'Earl of Dudley's Mines Map, 1812', where it is named and shown as a water mill.

In 1818 we find John Fisher listed as corn miller of Great Bridge.[5] James Fisher died in the following year.

By 1828 a rival firm had sprung up,[6] for we find not only John Fisher of Great Bridge but Henry Nock of Great Bridge listed as millers.

This state did not last long, for in 1829 there appears the entry 'Fisher and Nock, Great Bridge'.[7] By 1835 Fisher had departed and in 1841 Henry Nock was operating 'Great Bridge Mill'.[8]

By 1850 Samuel Nock was the miller at Great Bridge flour mill.[9] He continued until 1854 after which date there is no further reference to this mill in the directories.

It is highly probable that this mill operated by water power for a short period only as most of the rival establishments which sprang up in this locality from 1810 to 1850 were steam-driven. It is not possible to identify positively this mill on the Dawson map of 1816 nor on the first edition of the 1in. O.S. map, 1834, though by the latter date the construction of the canal arm in this area had modified the bed of the river.

NOTES

1. F. W. Hackwood, *History of Tipton* (1891), p. 21.
2. William Salt Library, Stafford; 67/22, Bundle 20.
3. *Plan of Fisher Estates*, undated; Tipton Central Library.
4. *West Bromwich Inclosure Map*, 1801-4.
5. *Parson and Bradshaw Directory of Staffordshire* (1818).
6. *Pigot's National and Commercial Directory* (1828).
7. *Pigot's Commercial Directory of Birmingham* (1829).
8. *Pigot's National and Commercial Directory* (1841).
9. *Slater's National and Commercial Directory* (1850).

XXX

SHEEPWASH MILL
(Grete or Greet Mill)

The Sheepwash Mill (973922) though non-existent at the
time of Domesday, was probably one of the oldest in
the district, certainly dating back to the 12th century.
Our first documentary evidence of it dates from about
1180[1] when 'Gervasse Paganelli, domini Honoris de Dudley'
confirmed the gift of his knight, 'William, son of Guy
of Offney' (then holder of the manor of West Bromwich)
of property to the Benedictine order for the founding
of the Sandwell Priory. This excellent, detailed deed
specifically names the 'Molendinum apud Grete'. The
site of the mill must have been somewhat unusual at
that time, for it was in an area devoid of population, so
far as we can tell, and at least a mile away from the 12th
century settlements which were to form parts of the
later West Bromwich and Tipton. Its only advantage of
site would seem to be the proximity of a river crossing
on which track routes from West Bromwich, Oldbury,
Dudley, Tipton and Wednesbury converged. Land in
this area, as far as possible from the manor houses of
both Tipton and West Bromwich, was some of the first
to be alienated from the respective manorial holdings and
it is scarcely surprising that within a century or two later,
a hamlet, the hamlet of Great (Grete) Bridge, had
sprung up close to the crossing.

What kind of work was carried out at such a remote
mill is a matter for conjecture, though with the clearing
of the woods and the development of the farming community, it seems probable that it was a corn mill by
the early 16th century.[2] It almost certainly remained

priory property throughout the interval. The 'Taxatio Ecclesiastica P. Nicholai IV' in 1291, stated that the Priory of Sandwell held 'duo molend. p. ann. xs.', that is, the mill at the priory and the one at Grete.[3]

Three years later in 1294, that litigious cleric, Thomas, Prior of Sandwell, was suing Nicholas Comitassone of Grete for one mill and half an acre of land in West Bromwich and Tipton.[4] We are not informed how the property came to be in the hands of Nicholas, but as he failed to answer the case, verdict was found for the Prior. The case seems to have caused some suspicion, for it was raised again two years later under the Statute of Mortmain. However the jury found for the Prior, declared that there was no evidence of collusion between the parties and that the property had belonged to the Priory since the endowment by William fitz Guy in the reign of Henry III. Incidentally, this finding would place the date of the gift somewhat later, at least 20 years, than our earlier estimate.

Another document of this time, sometime between 1272 and 1296, makes reference to the mill. 'Grant by Richard de Marnham, Lord of Bromwych, with the assent of Margery, his wife to Robert de Grete, for his homage and service and for 5 marks beforehand, of his part of a Ley in W. Bromwych, late of William de Wavere, between the part of that Ley of Walter de Evereas adjoining the highway from Bromwych Church to Grete Mill at the yearly rent of 4s. saving foreign service and two suits of his court at the Courts next after Michaelmas and 'le Hokeday'.[5]

From that time there is no mention of the Greet Mill for about 450 years, and it is probable that it fell into decay. The name was used for the 'Izon's Mill' (*q.v.*) during the 18th century, and probably earlier.

It is certain that the Priory had ceased to own this mill by the time of the Dissolution in 1526, since the two mills that were in priory possession at that date were Sandwell and Jone Mills (*q.v.*).[6]

We can find no evidence of the use of this site until the 18th century. The fact that a mill and a dam from which it obtained its power did not necessarily stand on properties both owned by the same landlord may be a possible explanation for the following. In 1739, Joseph Young of 'Ship Wash' was paying Joseph Jesson an annual rent of 5s. 0d. 'for Pounding ye Water upon a peice of Land that Hum. Whild holds'.[7] In 1762 Jesson noted that he received of Mr. William Holden via Mr. Hesekiah Smith, £6 6s. for two years' rent, 'for Pounding the Water upon my Land by meanes of which the Land is Wash'd away and the Brook is Widond'. Which of these men were tenants of the land and which operators of the mill is uncertain.

An abstract of deeds from 1713 to 1816 dealing with the ownership of a parcel of land in the Great Bridge area, defines it as adjacent to the lane leading from Greets Green towards the 'Blade Mill at Sheepwash', i.e. Sheepwash Lane.[8]

In 1798, Yates marked the mill on his map as being on the river. Dawson's map of 1816 gives no indication of the mill or a mill pool, yet it must have been still in existence. The 1in. O.S. map of 1831, while not very clear, does suggest that the river was dammed to form a pool just before passing under the canal arm which was constructed between 1816 and 1830. Describing the course of the Tame at this point, Reeves, stated that the river passed 'Gutteridge's Mill and Sheepwash Mill, passes under the canal and Great Bridge and divides Tipton and Wednesbury from West Bromwich'.[9]

According to the local rate books in 1813 Thomas Smith was paying a rate of 18s. 1½d. for Sheepwash Mill.[10] The following year the site was recorded as vacant. By 1819 Thomas Law of Sheepwash was paying 4s. 2d. for the house and 8s. 4d. for the mill. By 1821 these had been taken over by Benjamin Hunt and Co. who continued to pay 8s. 4d. for a number of years. In 1834 Benjamin Hunt was named as a manufacturer of bar and round iron at the 'Sheepwash Mill'.[11] Two years later, in 1836, Reeves stated that it had been a wire-mill but was then derelict, the 'remnants' being visible at that time.[12] It is probable that this marked the end of the use of the water mill. It would seem however that it was replaced by a much larger manufactory for Benjamin Hunt was paying a greatly increased rate for an ironworks in Sheepwash from 1836 until 1851, the firm ceasing to operate in the following year.

Parkes, writing in 1913, tells us that 'such a mill was actually in working order recently [he does not say how recently] for slitting nail rods, near Sheepwash Lane, and in close proximity to Denbigh Hall'.[13] He adds 'as late as 1870 the large supply pool was utilised for boating purposes'. It is strange that such does not appear on any of the later maps.

In recent years the river course has been scoured and straightened, the canal infilled and the site used as a corporation tip.

NOTES

1.   M. Willett, *op. cit.*, pp. 145-6.
2.   *Ibid.*, pp. 164-224.
3.   Stebbing Shaw, *op. cit.*, vol. 1, p. xxi.
4.   *Plea Roll*, 1294 (*S.H.C.*, vol. VII, pt. 1, p. 18).
5.   Catalogue of Ancient Deeds; C 4405.
6.   P.R.O., E 36/165, f. 132.
7.   Jesson Account Books; Jesson Deeds, No. 119.
8.   William Salt Library, Stafford; 67/22, Bundle 20.
9.   Jos. Reeves, *op. cit.*, pp. 5-6.
10. Tipton Rate Books.
11. *White's Staffordshire Directory* (1834).
12. Jos. Reeves, *op. cit.*, p. 114.
13. J. Parkes, *op. cit.*, p. 27.

XXXI

DUNKIRK MILL

About a mile downstream from 'The Mill' was the site of Dunkirk Mill, another source of water power which played its part in local life for over 300 years. Lying within a meander of the Tame, the mill drew its water from a shallow pool, bounded by an extensive earth bank, and supplied from the river where it was controlled by a system of weirs and sluices. It was the last of the old mills to surrender to the demands of the iron industry, some 30 years later even than Izon's Mill.

Like a number of its fellows, the earliest records of its existence date from the late 16th century, though it may already have been old by that time. It was then owned by Robert Ryder.

Ryder (with variant spellings) had been a family name in West Bromwich since the 1380 Poll Tax, when Nicholas of that name, a farmer, and Christiana, his wife, were assessed at 2s.[1] The various records which contain the name, other than this one, give no hint as to occupation, nor until 1527, of the family place of residence. A deed of that date, refers to 'the highway from Robert Rider's house to the town of Dudley . . . close to the water called the Tame'.[2] This might well be taken to be evidence that the family was already settled in Greet at or near to the site of the Dunkirk Mill.

The first member of the family whom we can definitely associate with this mill was another Robert, active in the latter part of the 16th century. His name appears in many deeds of the period 1573-7. As the family was connected with the mill for well over a hundred years, it might well make our story a little clearer if we look at the part of the Ryder family tree for this period.

Robert, who died in 1579, was succeeded by his 21-year-old son, Simon, destined to be the best-known member of the family. Simon was at that time living at Oldbury at or near to his in-laws. He had married, the year before, Margaret, daughter of Nicholas and Margery Smith, at Halesowen church, since Oldbury was at that time part of the parish of Halesowen. With his wife and children, Nicholas and Joanne, he took up his residence in West Bromwich on 4 June 1580, though we cannot be sure whether it was actually at the mill or at the house later to be called Dunkirk Hall, which was built about this time and the remains of which, much altered, form the *Dunkirk* Inn, in Whitehall Road, West Bromwich, of today.

Simon Ryder, like his father before him, was a remarkable man in his day. A literate man, he wrote fluently in both English and Latin, using a very legible 'court hand', and had at least some acquaintance with Greek. His knowledge of law enabled him to argue successfully his case before the courts. A farmer, miller and landowner, he from time to time acted as recorder at the Manorial Courts of West Bromwich, Oldbury and Walloxhall, and even Halesowen. His services were in considerable demand to witness documents and legal procedures, and to act as assessor in disputes between his neighbours, which is a reflection of the esteem in which he was held. Like his father, he kept a note book, in which, from time to time, throughout his life, he recorded matters which interested him. Unfortunately, Robert Ryder's book no longer exists, but that of Simon, which he entitled *Hypomnema,* now in the William Salt Library, survives, providing most interesting details of social life in this area in late Tudor and early Stuart times.

Simon's entry into his father's estate was not without problems, for four months later, October 1579, he appeared before the West Bromwich Court of Mistress Winifred Stanley, lady of the manor, presided over by

Family of **RYDER** (Rider) of Dunkirk

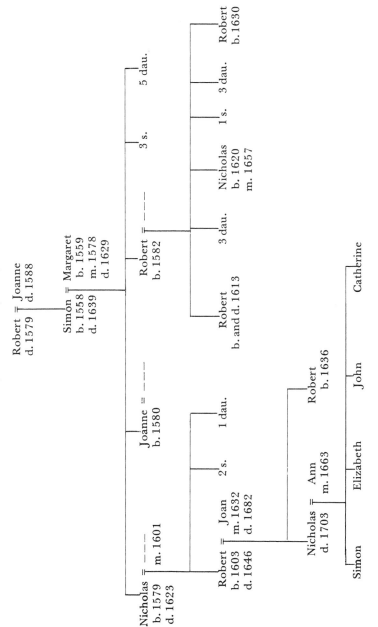

her steward, William Booth, to show cause why he should not pay heriot on coming into the property, in other words that the estate was not a copyhold part of the manorial holding.[3] This he did by quoting deeds back to 1324, when the land had been alienated by the then lady of the manor, Margery Marnham, to Walter Erdington, on payment of an annual chief rent and service. This plea was accepted and Simon then appeared at the manorial court of a year later to agree as to his 'service' which was fixed at a 'tenth of a knight's fee' but without homage. He continued to pay chief rent, which was fixed at 14d. for many years, as is witnessed by numerous entries in his note book, such as that for 21 May 1630.[4]

The family were staunch Catholics and as such were subject to official displeasure both during the reign of Elizabeth and again during the Commonwealth. In 1598, the Sheriff and his men arrived in West Bromwich to distrain on the goods of Simon Ryder, recusant.[5] This provoked something of an uproar in the locality, resulting in some 37 people, including Simon's widowed mother-in-law, Margery Smith, his son Nicholas, and daughter Joan, appearing at Stafford Assizes charged with riotous assembly and assault on the Sheriff's officers. Some of the accused, in their turn, brought charges of assault against the same men. We are not informed of the result of the cases and Simon himself makes no reference to it. Only briefly does he state 'my mill was burned the 22nd., day of Aprill Anno dni 1600 et Ao Eliz 42'.[6] Whether this was the result of another disturbance or an accident we shall never know. A few years later, when the 1604 survey of Catholics was made, it was recorded that West Bromwich contained 'many popish', but only three are named: Simon Ryder, Margaret his wife, and Alice, wife of William Sheppard.[7]

The mill was rebuilt and Simon decided to employ a miller. He records the conditions of employment. 'Mo. that owen davies cam to me to dwell the 28th day of Maie being fridai in Whitsonweek Anno dni 1602 et Ao. Eli. 44 and must have 45s. a yeare, a shirt, s----, thrid [thread?] and lingells [leather straps] and must not be sett to anie outworke from the mille unlesse in tyme of great need in harvest about hey or corne or amending the mille damme or about the fludgates or mill and must bestowe the rest of his tyme att the mille about his owne worke and commoditie, keeping my mille in good and orderlie sorte'.[8]

For some reason Simon appears to have given up the more strenuous part of his farming when he was in his mid-40s, for from that time he rented much of his land to others[9] and in 1603-4 sold some of his cattle, his team (of oxen?) and 'my waine [four-wheeled wagon], tumbrells [two-wheeled carts], plows, cheines, yokes and such like' to his son Nicholas, who was to pay partly by instalments and partly by work.

As the mill owner, he retained his interest in the control of the Tame. In 1607, he assisted in bringing two of his neighbours to an agreement as to the use of the water.[10] William Sheppard was to construct a trough (or sluice) and gate by which the water level could be maintained a foot or so below ground level and by which his water-meadow could be flooded at will.

In addition to the aforementioned chief rents on his properties, Simon had to pay 'Easter Tithes'. In 1621, these amounted to 3s. for his household and 2s. for his mill.[11]

The year 1625 brought an event in the life of the mill, for new millstones were fitted.[12] This pair of stones was purchased from John Amerie for £6 15s. It is interesting to speculate as to their origin. Were they of Pennine grit or the poorer Bilston sandstone? The high price suggests the former. They were hauled on a wagon pulled by a team of 16 oxen and supervised by three men on horseback. It must have created a sensation locally.

In 1632, Robert Ryder, son and heir of Nicholas, who had died nine years previously, married Joan Sydenhall.[13] Four fields, close to the mill, sold to Nicholas by Simon in 1604, were included in the marriage settlement. Soon after this, Simon, now a widower of 74, went to live with his grandson Robert, paying 50s. a quarter for his lodging but in turn charging him rent for some of the land he owned.[14] It is uncertain whether they were then living in Simon's old home, Dunkirk Hall, or that which had been the home of Nicholas. It may have been that Nicholas had used part of his father's house and not a separate establishment.

From 1632 onwards the note book contains only entries relating to rents. Such entries continue in Simon's hand until December 1639 two months prior to his death, the estate then devolving on grandson Robert. When he died in 1646 the estate was managed by his widow Joan, his two children being under age at the time. Her name appears with those of 21 others listed as recusants in West Bromwich in 1657.[15] There were six other Ryders listed. Her name also appears in the manorial rent roll of 1649.

The estate was eventually taken over by her son, Nicholas. In 1663, he married Ann Palin and the marriage settlement included the house, outbuildings, orchards and mill, 'commonly called Ryder's Mill', and names 17 fields.[16] Hackwood suggests that it was at this time that the brick front part of the Hall was added to the earlier half-timber structure which lay behind.[17] He gives this as an instance of extravagances which were to bring problems. However the house was not very large by 1666, when Nicholas was taxed for three hearths which was less than the miller's house at Bustleholme.[18] Two other Ryders, his uncle John (one hearth) and cousin Richard (three hearths) appear in the same taxation list.

Nicholas Ryder did not operate the mill himself but leased it out on a monthly rental. It is difficult to see how the rent was assessed as in the four months from July 1672 it fluctuated from 18s. 4d. to 19s., rather odd amounts.[19] In the following year the rent was evened up to level shillings but still it varied from 10s. in July to £1 10s. in November. It may be that the rent was a reflection of monthly turnover.

Twenty years later, Nicholas was in serious financial difficulties and mortgaged parts of the property in 1691, 1693 and 1694.[20] When he died in 1703 the estate was in debt and his executors, Thomas Whitgreave, Gilbert Merry, Thomas Palin and John Pigeon were directed to sell it and arrange a settlement,[21] but disputes arose and by 1708 it became the subject of a very protracted case in Chancery, a case which was to drag on for about a century.

During this period this mill remained a corn mill. Writing in 1836, Reeves states that the family of Gutteridge had lived there for upwards of a hundred years.[22] The first mention of this family in the parish register is in 1731 and though we know little of them, they must have been of some significance in West Bromwich at that time, as operators of one of the only two corn mills working there. In 1737 the Parish Meeting was held at the home of Mr. Gutteridge.

The mill is marked on the maps of Staffordshire of W. Yates in 1775 and 1798.

In 1812, the estate was purchased by Messrs. Stansbie, Blount and Whitgreave[23] but four years later, when Stansbie became bankrupt in 1816, his share, including the mill, was sold to the brothers Thomas and Henry Price. For a time the mill continued in its old ways, for in 1818 it was worked by Daniel Gutteridge, 'farmer and miller'.[24] This must have marked the end of its existence as a corn mill, for by 1823 Thomas Price had converted it to a forge.[25] A directory of 1828 lists Thomas and Henry Price as manufacturers of pig iron, but such work was unlikely to have been on this site as we have no reference to a blast furnace here.[26] In 1834 Thomas Price is recorded as a manufacturer of iron rod. This tallies with the comment of Reeves in 1836 that 'a sample of the old school of making iron where the hammer is lifted by a water-wheel is Mr. Spencer's Mill formerly Gutteridge's Flour Mill'.[27] Spencer who took over the mill in 1835 was probably a lessee for Hackwood stated that 'the Trustees of the Price family, of whom John Walker Turton was one, eventually sold their third part of

the estate, including the old Mill and watercourse to
the Birmingham Canal Co., who are the present [1895]
owners'.[28] He added that Dunkirk Hall was then the
property of Alderman Reuben Farley. The mill remained
under the control of Spencers up to about 1850, at which
date they were operating the Vulcan Foundry and the
Dunkirk Forge.[29] A plan of the estate, drawn in 1838 by
Joseph Cooksey, gives the information that the extent of
the 'Dunkirk Forge etc., stream, road and water-power
apparatus belonging thereto was 4 acres 35 sq. yds.'.[30]

By 1856 it had become the Dunkirk Iron Foundry of
Nightingale and Co. though it is interesting to note that
it still appears on the West Bromwich Town Plan of 1857
as 'Gutteridge's Mill'.[31] Nightingale and Co. continued.
to work the foundry until 1862 when they moved to
Ryder's Green.[32]

The construction of the canal in 1828-30 and the railway in 1847 led to the reduction of the size of the dam
and the culverting of the Tame and the mill sluice
but appears not to have seriously affected the operation
of the mill. We cannot be certain that Nightingales any
longer used water-power in the work, but a series of
plans drawn between 1865 and 1868 show the forge
and the adjacent dam.[33] Another, dated 1872, names the
forge as 'Dunkirk Mill' alongside the dam.

At what time it ceased to exist is uncertain, but today
a marshy area is all that is left of the dam and a few
bricks mark the site of the one-time mill and forge.

NOTES

1.   *Poll Tax Roll*, 1380 (*S.H.C.*, vol. XVII, p. 170).
2.   F. W. Hackwood, *History of West Bromwich* (1895), p. 71.
3.   S. Rider, *Hypomnema* (1579-1639), p. 5. This is a MS.
diary and note book in the William Salt Library, Stafford.
4.   *Ibid.*, p. 95.
5.   *Staffordshire Quarter Session Rolls*, 1598 (*S.H.C.*, 1935,
pp. 40-41).
6.   S. Rider, *op. cit.*, p. 140.
7.   *Recusant Rolls*, 1590-3, with added statement, 1604
(*S.H.C.*, 1915, p. 387).

8. S. Rider, *op. cit.*, p. 70.
9. *Ibid.*, pp. 72-3.
10. *Ibid.*, p. 74.
11. *Ibid.*, p. 88.
12. *Ibid.*, p. 92.
13. M. Willett, *op. cit.*, p. 176.
14. S. Rider, *op. cit.*, p. 98.
15. *List of Recusants, 1657 (S.H.C.*, 1947, pt. 2, pp. 88-9).
16. M. Willett, *op. cit.*, p. 177.
17. F. W. Hackwood, *History of West Bromwich* (1895), p. 74.
18. *Staffordshire Hearth Tax*, 1666 (*S.H.C.*, 1923, p. 246).
19. S. Rider, *op. cit.*, p. 108.
20. M. Willett, *op. cit.*, p. 178.
21. As 17 above.
22. Jos. Reeves, *op. cit.*, p. 53.
23. As 20 above.
24. *Parson and Bradshaw's Staffordshire Directory* (1818).
25. Ward and Price, *New Birmingham Directory* (1823).
26. *Pigot's National and Commercial Directory* (1828).
27. Jos. Reeves, *op. cit.*, p. 114.
28. F. W. Hackwood, *History of West Bromwich* (1895), p. 75.
29. *Slater's National and Commercial Directory* (1850).
30. Jos. Cooksey, *Plan of Dunkirk Estate* (1838); MS. Tipton Library.
31. *Post Office Directory of Birmingham* (1856).
32. *Slater's Directory of the Midlands* (1862).
33. MS. Plans in Tipton Library.

XXXII

'THE MILL': TURTON'S, IZON'S OR GREET MILL

This, the next mill upstream (989905), is an ancient site, but one which yields no hint as to the reason for its location. Present-day examination of the area reveals no natural advantage on this site, but such is the change wrought upon the scene by the last two centuries that it is scarcely surprising.

While it is impossible to give an exact date for the original building, it was almost certainly very early in the 14th century. In 1301, William Geoffrey of Oldbury was accused of damage to the road leading from that village 'versus molendinum de Grete'.[1] Five years later the jury found that Thomas of Wednesbury, working the 'Grete-melne' was in the habit of opening the sluices at the Oldbury Mill to the detriment of the upper mill for the benefit of his 'Gretemulne'.[2]

It will be noted that the name Greet Mill had been used of the Sheepwash Mill (*q.v.*, p. 150), the property of the Sandwell Priory up to 1294, but it will be obvious from the above paragraph that, some 10 years later, the name was used for a mill much nearer to Oldbury than the Great Bridge one. In fact the 1306 reference is almost certainly to this Izon's (Greet) and Bromford (Oldbury) mills. The name Greet was used throughout the centuries for the area along the river from Bromford to Great Bridge.

The earliest certain date which can be placed on the two mills on this site is 1583, for in that year they were purchased by William Turton of West Bromwich and Thomas Cowper, *alias* Piddock, of Oldbury from John Skevynton, armiger.[3] As the Cowpers were people of some affluence in Oldbury, it is possible that he was the sleeping partner financing the transaction. Three years later, in 1586, Winifred Stanley, Lady of the Manor of West Bromwich, conveyed to William Turton 'the Watercourse or Mill Fleame in the Parish of West Bromwich so far as the waste ground etc.' with the liberty of scouring the same. The chief rent was to be one rose flower annually if demanded.[4] The partnership did not last long for Thomas Cowper conveyed the two mills (under one roof), one a corn mill and the other a blade-mill, together with the Floodgate Meadow and other property to William Turton, the elder, of West Bromwich in 1592.[5]

The Turton family owned the mills for about 150 years and during that period played such a part in local life that it is worth our while to look at the family tree or at least that part of it concerned with the mills.[6]

The family was typical of the growing 'middle-class' of their time, tradesmen fostering the infant industrial age. James states that they migrated from Lancashire,[7] while Hackwood claims that the grandfather of John Turton was living in Dudley.[8] Certain it is that the family had established themselves in the Oldbury area by the second half of the 16th century, as nail-masters trading in nail rod and, no doubt, the finished products.

As related above, William Turton acquired the two mills before the end of the century. This would indicate that already the Turtons had accumulated some wealth and that though William is referred to as a 'naylor', he certainly was not one of the poverty-stricken toilers who existed in such large numbers in the Black Country throughout the next 200 years. In fact further evidence of the financial standing of the family may be gathered from the will of William Turton the younger, who dying in 1621, in his father's lifetime, when he could not have yet inherited his father's property, bequeathed lands and estates in West Bromwich, King's Norton, Solihull, Tipton, Barre and Banbury and a 'blade Mill' and meadows in Oldbury.[9] We are not told how much of this was the marriage portion of his wife, but it is evident that he was a man of property.

Family of TURTON of West Bromwich

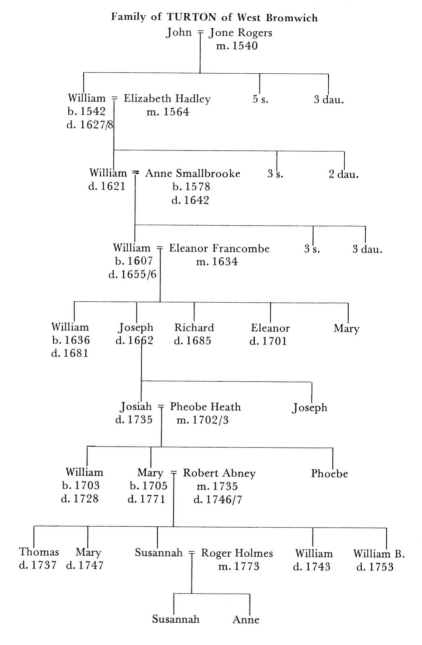

William Turton, the elder, the purchaser of the mills lived to the age of 85, dying in January 1627/8. There are extant several references to the purchase of land by him, usually in 'Greet', that part of the Tame valley between Oldbury and Great Bridge. Though no doubt farming on their own accounts, both he and his sons rented out part of their possessions, as is shown by the items for rent paid by Simon Ryder, his neighbour.[10] This landowner, farmer, manufacturer and merchant did not hesitate to contribute to the social life of this land in which he had settled. From 1602 for a number of years he represented West Bromwich on both Quarter Session Juries and Special Juries in the County.[11] He made practical attempts to alleviate the growing poverty in the town, for in 1615 he donated property including a cottage in Lyndon and fields in 'Pudding Land' in order to establish the 'Pudding Land Dole'.[12] The first trustees were William Turton the elder, and his sons, William, John, and Thomas.

Thomas became the founder of the Hateley Heath branch of the family, a branch which has no significance in our story of the mills. John, growing in substance, following his father's line of business, purchased the Oak House from his brother Thomas in 1633, thus acquiring the family home of his descendants: the branch of the family known as the 'Turtons of the Oak'.

As mentioned above, the eldest son, William the younger predeceased his father. He had married Anne Smallbrooke, daughter of a Birmingham ironmonger, and when William died in 1621, Anne was left a widow with seven children, the eldest boy, another William, being a scarce 14 years of age. Among other bequests, Anne was left specific amounts to provide for the maintenance and education of each of the sons. She carried out the instruction for we find that William matriculated at Oxford in 1624, and was intended, says tradition, for the legal profession, but on the death of his grandfather William in 1627/8, he inherited the mills and took on the family business, living at 'The Mill'. His mother, Anne, continued to take an active part in affairs until her death in 1642. In 1621, she received the rent for the 'tiath hay at Oldbury' from Simon Ryder.[13] In 1635 she purchased Brandford (Bromford) Leasow from William Cartwright of Oldbury.[14]

The Turton family appear to have avoided the worst effects of the Civil War. Certainly they escaped the fate of their fellow ironmongers and bladesmiths of Birmingham at the hands of Rupert's cavalry. Undoubtedly their sympathies, like those of their class in the Midlands, were with the Parliamentarians but they do not appear on the list of local active supporters in 1662, despite the participation of 'Col. Turton'.[15] At the same time they avoided the heavy penalties levied on their Royalist neighbours, the Whorwoods, who appear with the Stanleys and Ryders of West Bromwich in the list of recusants in 1657.[16] They were typical of the families who were to form the 'nonconformist, liberal industrialists' of the Birmingham of the 19th century. In 1635 another trust was formed to administer the 'Brick Kiln Dole', named from the lands which provided the funds, and again we find Turtons periodically as trustees.

In 1655/6, William of the mills died leaving a widow, Eleanor, née Francombe, three sons and two daughters. His eldest son and heir was yet another William, who in turn inherited these mills and lived at 'The Mill'. This was one of the larger houses of the district at that time, for in 1666, William was assessed for nine hearths.[17] This number was exceeded in West Bromwich only by the manor with 16 hearths, and his cousin's house, the 'Oake', with eleven. Throughout this period, the family continued to acquire property and the name of William Turton appears on many of the indentures but we cannot be sure that it was always William of 'the Mill' as William was a popular name in this, by now, widespread and numerous family. A list of recipients of the 'Podinland Dole' in 1677 and 1678, in the handwriting of Thomas Jesson, names 'William Turton of the Mill' as the benefactor.[18]

When William died, without issue, in 1681, the mills passed to the third son, Richard, the second, Joseph, being already dead.

Richard was a man of means, for in 1682, he joined with a kinsman, George Devenish, to lend a considerable sum to his cousin, William Turton of the 'Oake', to enable him to settle his affairs, on the security of a mill and lands in Kings Norton.[19] However, Richard did not long enjoy his inheritance for he died four years later in 1685. Our only record of him in the West Bromwich Manorial Court Rolls is that entry which records his death, seised of a messuage of mills and lands belonging to the same within the manor and stating that 'Elinor' Turton was his heiress.[20] Richard left no family, so the mills passed to his sister Eleanor.

For the 16 years which she occupied the mills, we have no records which tell us whether she continued the family business, dealing in iron and nails. In fact we know little of her but for the repeated entries in the manorial court rolls that Elinor Turton, spinster of the Mill, was one of the listed defaulters, i.e. she failed to appear at the court or plead excuse, for which on each occasion she was fined 2d. In her will she left £2 10s. annually each to the poor of West Bromwich and Oldbury, chargeable on the profits of the mill, thus continuing the family tradition of establishing charities.[21] In 1694 the Greet Mill was stated to be 'two ancient water corn-mills under one roof'.[22]

With the death of Eleanor in 1701, the family inheritance passed to her nephew, Josiah Turton, elder son of her deceased brother, Joseph. He continued to live at the 'Mill', which remained a corn mill, and carried on work as a farmer and ironmonger or nailer. In 1708 he purchased from John Shelton, lord of the manor, the two mill closes, adjacent to the lane leading from 'Josiah Turton's Corn Mill to Great Bridge'.[23] From time to time he bought rod iron from the Stour valley forges.[24] In 1722, his son William, then only 19 years of age, was appointed one of the trustees of the Pudding Land Dole.

Unfortunately, dying at the age of 25, William predeceased his father. Since William was an only son, the death of Josiah in 1735 brought an end to the association of the name of Turton with these mills. One item in the Chief Rent Roll of Samuel Clarke, for the year 1732-3[25] is 'Jos. Turton of ye Mill for Greet Mill and Greet Mill Meadow . . . 8d.'.

The property now descended to Mary, the elder of Josiah's two daughters. Shortly after her father's death she married Robert Abney. He proceeded to carry on the family business, buying his rod from time to time from the Stour valley forges up to the time of his death in 1746/7.[26] His widow continued the business for the rest of her life until 1771. Mrs. Abney paid 8d. Chief Rent 'for Greet's Mill & Meadow' from 1736 to 1760 at least.[27] It was during this time, in 1768-9 that Brindley constructed his canal from Birmingham to Wolverhampton with its branch to Wednesbury. This canal, passing within but yards of the mills, was to have a profound effect on the future of both. The headwaters of this branch of the Tame were amputated to provide the canal feeders for the topmost pound, leaving the mills largely dependant on the overflow weirs for their water supply. On the other hand the canal offered a vastly improved means of transport both for the obtaining of raw materials and the distribution of manufactured products. The first map of the Birmingham-Wednesbury Canal[28] names 'the Mill' as Mrs. Abney's Mill. This name was to cling for many years. Greenwood's map of Staffordshire, 1819, called it 'Abney's Old Mill' and in fact Teesdale's map of 1831 still referred to it as 'Abney's Mill'. Mrs. Mary Abney continued the charity, founded by her great-aunt, which now became known as the 'Abney Dole'. This dole was paid by successive occupants of the mill until well into the present century.

On her death in 1771, there was another change of name, for history repeated itself. She was survived by but one daughter, Susannah, who two years later married a Walsall lawyer, Roger Holmes.

The marriage of Susannah Abney to Roger Holmes in 1773 would appear to mark the end of the operation of the mills by the Turtons and their descendants and of their residence at the 'Mill' but not of their ownership. In the correspondence between Holmes and Matthew Boulton in 1774,[29] the former points out that he owns the land adjacent to the lower mill and could easily enlarge the mill-pool but would be restricted in water supply to the overflow from the canal weir and from the upper pool. We have no evidence that he did in fact enlarge the pool. He leased the mill, pool and house for a short period. One of the tenants was certainly a Mr. Hawkes. In 1778, he advertised as to let on lease, 'The Mill Estate lying in West Bromwich and Oldbury, about 75 acres, chiefly meadowing . . . and a set of overshut water corn mills thereon'.[30] The property also included the Bromford Forge, fishery in pools and canal, the main house with walled garden, three fish stews, two summer houses and a greenhouse. In the issue of Aris's *Birmingham Gazette* for 7 October 1782 there appeared the following advertisement:

> Lands and Water Mill to be let from Lady Day next, the Mill Estate lying in West Bromwich and Oldbury (about five and a half miles from Birmingham, the same from Walsall and three from Dudley) containing about 75 acres and a set of overshut water corn mills thereon, now in the tenure of Mr. Thomas Hawkes.
>
> N.B. The above set of mills stand very near the Birmingham Navigation, and are now in use for grinding corn and dressing leather, and are in an eligible situation for these purposes or for the Birmingham Manufactories. Mr. John Sedgley will show the premises and for particulars enquire of Mr. Holmes, Park Street, Walsall.

This advertisement confirms the continued association of this mill with its rural origins. In fact it is the only reference we have to a mill in this area being used for leather-dressing. It is surprising that it was powered by 'overshot' wheels, for there is little fall on this section of the river and the pool was constructed by building an earth bank around a field, which must have been almost flat.

The proximity of the canal is probably the most important fact mentioned. It was probably this that attracted the 'Birmingham Manufactories' and brought to an end its long history as a corn mill. The Birmingham firm of Izon and Whitehouse, manufacturers of hinges and other hardware, took the lease of the mill and set up a foundry. W. E. Jephcott informs us that 'the mill machinery, hitherto used for grinding corn, was adapted for its new purpose. The mill wheel drove a square wooden shaft which was rounded where the wooden block bearings supported it. The whole of the pulleys in the turning shop were made of solid wood and the insides of the kettles and saucepans were turned by a tool held in the workman's hand.'[31] Water power was now proving inadequate and in 1785 there appeared in Aris's *Birmingham Gazette* a notice to the effect that 'the owners and occupiers of works on the River Tame or on the streams that flow into the river are desired to meet at the Hotel in Birmingham to consider what steps it may be necessary to take to preserve the streams they have hither to enjoyed'. Izon and Whitehouse took their own steps for they installed a Boulton and Watt steam-engine.[32] It is probable that this was a second-hand one purchased from Jesson and Wright (*see* Bromford Mill) since this firm appears in Boulton's Sales Book, while Izons do not. From this time on to the present day the foundry has been known as Izons. A map of 1795 '25 miles round Birmingham' shows the site as Izon's Works. This, however, does not denote ownership.

Hackwood asserts that on the death of Roger Holmes, the property should have passed to his two daughters, but as they were both mentally deranged, it eventually went to a distant relative after lengthy Chancery proceedings.[33] This state of the two daughters is repeated by James (*op. cit.*). It is difficult to reconcile this with other sources. Unfortunately the mill itself does not appear in the West Bromwich Enclosure maps, 1801-04, but adjoining land does and it is marked as belonging to 'Miss Holmes', not an administrator or trustee.

3:   Izon's Foundry, *c.* 1820

The Churchwarden's Book for 1815 acknowledges the receipt from Miss Holmes of £2 10s. for the (Abney) dole.

The tithe schedule of 1849 shows the foundry, house and some 30 acres of land as belonging to Mr. Edward Holmes and leased by Mr. Izons.

The installation of the engine referred to above meant the end of water power but the pool was retained as a source of water for the engine and purposes of the foundry, the stream being finally diverted in 1906-7.[34] The old house remained standing, used as a store, until 1941.

NOTES

1. Halesowen Manorial Court Rolls, *Trans. of Worcs. Hist. Soc.*, vol. 1, p. 428.

2. *Ibid.*, p. 584.

3. *Final Concord*, 1582 (*S.H.C.*, vol. XV, p. 149).

4. P.R.O., C 103/40 Sheet 1.

5. S. Rider, *op. cit.*, pp. 51-2.

6. C. S. James, *The Turton Family* (1927); E. Lissimore, *West Bromwich Inhabitants*, undated bound MS., West Bromwich Reference Library.

7. *Ibid.*

8. F. W. Hackwood, *History of West Bromwich* (1895), p. 63.

9. Chas. H. Bayley, *Extracts from the Will of William Turton, the Younger* (1837), MS. in West Bromwich Reference Library.

10. S. Rider, *op. cit.*, p. 90.

11. *Staffordshire Jury Lists*, 1602 onwards (*S.H.C.*, 1935 and 1940).

12. M. Willett, *op. cit.*, p. 139.

13. As 10 above.

14. M. Willett, *op. cit.*, p. 167.

15. List of active parliamentarians, 1662 (*S.H.C.*, 1947, pt. 2, p. 63).

16. *List of Recusants*, 1657 (*S.H.C.*, 1947, pt. 2, pp. 88-9).

17. *Staffordshire Hearth Tax*, 1666 (*S.H.C.*, 1923, p. 246).

18. Jesson Deeds, No. 57.

19. M. Willett, *op. cit.*, p. 165.

20. West Bromwich Manorial Court Roll, 1685.

21. W. E. Jephcott, *House of Izons* (1948), p. 12.

22. P.R.O., C 5/188/39.

23. M. Willett, *op. cit.*, p. 201.

24. Knight's Account Books.

25. Stafford County Record Office, D(W)627(A)30.

26. Knight's Account Books.

27. Stafford County Record Office, D(W)628(A)30-630(A)30. P.R.O., C 103/127, 28/9.

28. Map of Birmingham Navigation, *Gentlemen's Magazine* (1771).

29. Boulton Correspondence, Birmingham Assay Office.

30. Aris's *Birmingham Gazette*, 9 February 1778.

31. W. E. Jephcott, *op. cit.*, p. 13.

32. *Ibid.*, p. 14.

33. F. W. Hackwood, *History of West Bromwich* (1895), p. 64.

34. As 32 above.

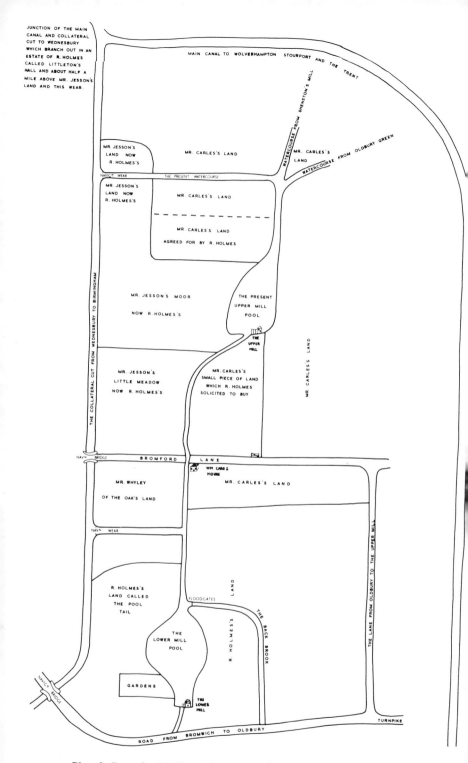

Plan 6: Bromford Mill and 'The Mill'. (Roger Holmes' Sketch Map, 1774.)

XXXIII

BROMFORD MILL

The Bromford Mill, on the north-flowing upper stream of the Tame (995901), to the west of West Bromwich, was situated near to the Bromford Lane, the West Bromwich to Oldbury road, at the crossing of the river. Here the slopes of each bank are somewhat steeper and the valley sides closer than in other parts of the adjacent stretch. Though this would appear to be the most convenient site for the construction of a dam, yet this was the only one such built within a mile or so.

As in the case of most other mills in this part of the world, little definite is known of it prior to the 16th century. We do know that mills existed in the Oldbury area at lease as early as the 13th century, but we cannot be certain of the exact sites of these. In 1272, 'Bromwich Mill' was let to Henry the Miller.[1] This mill was quite possibly on the Bromford site, since that is on the West Bromwich-Oldbury boundary. In 1301, litigation arose when Thomas of Wednesbury, holder of the 'Greet Mill', made a practice of opening the sluices of the Oldbury Mill, higher up the stream, to turn his own wheels.[2] The position of Bromford and Greet mills strongly suggests that they may have been the two concerned in the activities of Thomas. However, we must remember that there were already, c. 1275, two other pools, one a vivarium or fish-stew, and the other a 'waspol' (washpool), in Oldbury, either of which might have been supplying power for a mill.

Hackwood asserts that 'Oldberrie Mill' with its appurtenant land was held by the Turtons of West Bromwich in the reign of Queen Elizabeth at a rent of 'xxd. a yeare'.[3]

Again, we cannot be sure that this mill and Bromford Mill are identical, but the fact that William Turton was soon to purchase the latter, makes it appear a probability. A reference to 'the lane from Grete Green to Oldbury Mill' in 1573 would seem to support a claim that the two names referred to the same mill.[4]

The mill was purchased in 1610 by William Turton, the younger (*see* p. 180) as part of the manor of Oldbury and Walloxhall, and when he sold the manor, seven years later, he kept the mill, then working as a blade-mill, together with four acres of meadow and a small close.[5] In 1620 he purchased additional adjacent lands from John and Richard Dudley, including one known as 'Smythie Leasow'.[6] These purchases seem to have been made in order to control 'all manner of pooles, stagnes, waters, lands and watercourses' and so ensure the supplies to the Bromford Mill.

After the death of William the younger, in 1621, the mill passed successively through the hands of his son William, grandson William and grand-daughter Eleanor.[7] In 1693, Joseph Carles (Carless) of Birmingham, a whitesmith, purchased the blade-mill and adjacent Leasow, in the manor of Oldbury, Walloxhall.[8] He pulled down the blade-mill and rebuilt it as an 'iron-forge or flatting mill'. This required more power than the previous blade-mill and he enlarged the mill-pool, diverting some of the headwaters. In 1694, Eleanor Turton, who had retained the Greet Mill, protested that when Carless was not working the Bromford Mill the water by-passed her mill, and when he was operating, the water came down to her mill in such quantities as to flood her pool and damage the floodgates.[9]

The Carless family owned Bromford for over 70 years. In the middle of the 18th century it was being worked by Edward Gibbons as a plating-forge, but in 1765, at which time it was untenanted, it was re-purchased by Mary Abney, great-niece of Eleanor Turton, living at the Greet Mill. She let the mill the same year to William Taylor.[10]

On the death of Mary Abney in 1770 the mills became the property of her daughter Susannah who married the Walsall lawyer, Roger Holmes, in 1773. Bromford was once more a grinding-mill in 1772.[11]

In September 1774, Roger Holmes wrote to Matthew Boulton[12] proposing a scheme for increasing the size of the dams at both mills and hence the available water supply. He even suggested rebuilding and enlarging the Bromford Mill, which was at that time occupied by a Mr. Carles. However, the scheme came to little, though the dam was extended somewhat by flooding the 'Moor' between the old dam and the canal, for the day of steam was about to dawn and the age of water power was coming to an end.

In 1778, Holmes advertised it to let, together with 'The Mill' as 'another Water-work near thereto and upon the same stream and called Bromford Forge'.[13]

Mr. Jephcott refers to 'an engraving of 1780 which shows a wire-mill driven by a water wheel' which appeared in an account of Bromford Ironworks, published 1923.[14] From the same account we learn that Mrs. Elizabeth Dawes, proprietress in 1887, claimed that the firm was then 100 years old, having been founded about 1787 by John Dawes. She further stated that he was partnered by a member of the Jesson family and that the firm became known as Jesson and Dawes. There may be some confusion about this. Samuel Dawes was the son-in-law of Richard Jesson, the senior partner of the firm of Jesson and Wright who operated the Old Forge slitting-mill (*q.v.*) at the end of the 18th century. As stated in the chapter on that mill, the firm had taken over the Bromford Mill by the turn of the century, when it was known as the ironworks of Wright and Jesson.[15] The 'Jesson and Dawes' period would seem to lie between this date and about 1818 when the firm was S. and J. Dawes. It should be pointed out that by this time main works had been built on the West Bromwich side of the canal and this probably marked the abandonment of the water mill site. The removal of the industry did not mean the sale of the site, for in 1801, the pool, moor and little meadow were the property of Miss Holmes.[16] They still had a part to play, for in 1849,[17] when they were the property of Edward Holmes, they were rented by J. Izon and the pool no doubt used to augment the supply to the lower pool, which was at that time being used by Izon's Foundry mainly to supply water for the engine. The construction of the railway, which was opened in 1851, brought the end nearer, for the line on its embankment crossed the site cutting the pool in two. The smaller part between the railway and the canal was eventually filled in and the level of the ground raised to provide space for the railway goods yard. The larger part beyond the railway lay close to the Broadwell Road and was drained and became the site of the Oldbury Carriage and Wagon Works. The ironworks continued to be operated by the Dawes family until May 1887.

NOTES

1.　Halesowen Manorial Court Rolls (1270), *Trans. Worcs. Hist. Soc.*, vol. 1, p. 7.

2.　*Ibid.*, p. 548.

3.　F. W. Hackwood,*Oldbury and Roundabout* (1915),p.82.

4.　West Bromwich Manorial Court Roll, 1573.

5.　Stafford County Record Office, D 707/17/3, pp. 15-16 and 32-3.

6.　Warley Library; MS. document No. 1.

7.　P.R.O., C 142/390/153; Prob. 11/137 (P.C.C., 57 Dale).

8.　Birmingham Reference Library, 324254.

9.　P.R.O., C 5/188/39.

10.　Stafford County Record Office, D 707/17/3, pp. 19, 21, 32-3;*Ibid.*, Q/SB A.1781; R. Whitworth, *Plan of Intended Navigation from Birmingham*, 1767.

11.　Stafford County Record Office, D 707/17/3, pp. 15-6.

12.　Boulton Correspondence, Birmingham Assay Office.

13.　Aris's *Birmingham Gazette*, 9 February 1778.

14.　W. E. Jephcott, *Old West Bromwich* (17 March 1944), Scrap Book, No. 7, West Bromwich Reference Library.

15.　West Bromwich Inclosure Award Map, 1801-4.

16.　*Ibid.*

17.　West Bromwich Tithe Map, 1849.

XXXIV

THE OLDBURY MILLS
Langley Mill, Oldbury Mill, Blackley (Blakeley) Mill, Shenston's Mill, Hill's Mill

During the last two centuries the area of Oldbury and Langley has become so confused through the construction of canals, roads and railways and through industrial development that it is very difficult to trace the exact courses of the earlier streams and thus to locate the sites of the mills. However, the close examination of some of the older maps, particularly the Oldbury and Langley Tithe map of 1845, together with a detailed study of the topography as it is today, offer some possible solution. There seem to have been three streams uniting to form the headwaters of the Tame in this area. The first, rising near to Whiteheath, flowed north and then north-east to cross the Oldbury-Halesowen road at Church Bridge (988893). It was joined at Oldbury Green by another stream which had originated in the Titford area, flowed north-east to Langley and then northwards to Oldbury Green. From this point it continued northward to a point near Broadwell Road (993899) where it was joined by another brook, which, rising from several springs in the Roebuck Lane and Spon Lane areas, took a course westward along a line followed later by the canal. The confluence of the streams marked the position of the mill-pool of the Bromford Mill (*q.v.*).

Further examination reveals three possible mill sites on these streams, three sites which receive some documentary support. These sites are (a) (996897) where stood the Blackley Mill; (b) (994884) in Langley; and (c) (991893) near to Oldbury Green. It is not possible always to associate one piece of information with a particular mill in this area. As a consequence it will be necessary to present all the quotations in chronological order irrespective of the mill referred to.

At the time of Domesday there were 13 berewicks, one of which was Oldbury, in the possession of the Bishop of Chester. There existed one mill but it is not possible to state in which of the 13 it was placed.

By the middle of the next century, Oldbury, together with a number of adjacent vills, was counted as part of the manor of Hales, which formed a major part of the possessions of the Abbey of Hales, the present Halesowen.

Before the end of that century a number of mills, belonging to that Abbey, had been erected in the area and let out at a rental to the operating millers. We are told that in 1275 a new pool was made between Wallockshale (Langley) and Oldbury where there already existed two pools.[1] The most likely site, from this description, would be the one suggested a little above Oldbury Green.

In 1293, John, son of Walter of Oldbury, came to the court and swore allegiance to the Abbot and agreed on a rental to be paid for a piece of land.[2] In return he was exempted from service other than mill suit.

A mill existed at 'Abbeleye' in or near to Oldbury in the following year, when Philip, son of Thomas of Oldbury agreed to allow a watercourse from this mill, property of the Abbot, to be made across his meadow;[3] 'Memorandum quod Philippus filius Thome de Oldbure concessit domino Abbate cursum aqua ad Molendinum de Abbeleye quod . . . est villate de Oldbure ut aqua predicta cursum suum in perpetuum habet per medium pratum suum sine impedimento'. It is not possible now to discover where this site, which appears to be a new one or a repaired one, was.

Shortly afterwards in 1297 a law case arose involving two apprentices at Oldbury Mill, as a result of Thomas, miller of Oldbury, borrowing a brass pot from Julia, daughter of John of Wallockshale.[4]

Life at the mills was certainly not dull in those days, for in 1306 the jury of 12 found that Thomas of Wednesbury, operator of the Greet Mill, was guilty of opening the sluices of the Oldbury Mill and letting out the water, to the detriment of the said Oldbury Mill and the advantage of his own Greet Mill.[5] Later the same year they found Thomas, son of John of Oldbury, guilty of poaching fish from the dam of 'Briddesmilne' approaching secretly through the hedges planted by the lord of the manor. They also stated that the way over the dam at Oldbury Mill was in disrepair by the fault of William the miller and fined him 12d., but this was later suspended when it was shown that the repair was in part the responsibility of the manor.[6]

The following year they found that William Geoffrey was responsible for the damage to the road from Oldbury leading to Greet Mill. The maintenance of the roads to the mills was obviously a matter of importance to the populace. In the next year, 1302, the jury stated that the road between the new mill and Oldbury was in such a state of dereliction by the fault of Henry de Hulle that it was a danger to travellers. He was ordered to put it in a state of repair by the following feast of St. Michael. Was this 'new mill' at Oldbury Green or is it possible that it was the first indication of the building of the Bromford Mill? It will be noticed that the previous jury verdict made no mention of this one at Bromford though the road from Oldbury to Greet Mill must have passed very close to the site.[7]

In the same year we find that the millers of Blakele, Walwyke and of the new mill were summoned to appear before the next court in order that they should take an oath to observe the manorial regulations as to the grinding of malt (brasii).[8] This entry is interesting in that it is the first reference that we have which details the work of the mills. It is also the first reference to the mill at Blackley, the site near to the Blackley Hall which we have allocated to the 'Oldbury Mill'. We believe that they were one and the same mill. Hackwood states that 'the Manor house, known as Blakeley [Blackley] Hall, situated in Oldbury, had attached to its gardens etc. . . . Also the water corn mills called Oldbury Mills and the millpool thereto belonging.[9]

It is a great pity that the Halesowen Court Rolls are not available for years after 1302, for I am certain that much valuable information would be obtained from such. As it is, we have to move forward some 250 years.

In 1573 Thomas Maire and William Curtler were ordered to scour their ditches in the lane leading from 'Grete Grene' towards Oldbury Mill before the feast of St. John the Baptist next.[10] Again we see the insistence on the maintenance of the mill roads.

There exists a copy of a fragment of a rent roll of West Bromwich Manor.[11] It is not dated, but from internal evidence must have been between 1585 and 1599. It is a list of Chief Rents and contains the item 'William Turton junior for Hadley's Land at Oldberie Mill. xxd.'. It should be noticed that this rent was for the land and not for the mill. The Bromford Mill was purchased in 1610 by William Turton the younger (*see* p. 174). Elsewhere there appears to have been confusion over both mills and persons.

For the next hundred years our evidence depends on a number of documents which supply information by inference rather than directly on the mills. An indenture of 1620 conveys from John and Richard Dudley to William Turton the younger, a number of pieces of land.[12] A house and four parcels of land are described as being adjacent to the king's highway leading from Oldburie to Millpoole Greene (Oldbury Green?). Another piece was described as 'one close of lands, meadow and pasture called and known by the name of the Smythie leasowe, now or late in the tenure of Thomas Hadley, lying in Oldburie and between . . . and the said Waterie Layne'. This land may well be the same referred to in the rent roll above, though it may be that they were two pieces, one each side of the river, that is, one in West Bromwich and one in Oldbury. In any case it seems that it was close to Bromford Mill, owned by Turton junior. William Turton the younger died in the following year, 1621.

The next indenture is a lease dated 1632, from the attorneys of John Dudley to William Cartwright and George Tonkes, of much the same pieces of land described in the 1620 lease.[13] It does contain reference to 'a certain furlonge there called Mill furlong' and to 'the comon there called Millpoole Greene'.

Of considerable interest is the Smethwick to Himley section of the Ogilby Strip map, 1675. It shows the relative positions of Oldbury, the Green, Blakeley Hall and Blakeley Mill.

Our next document, which would seem to refer to the same piece of land discussed above, is a copyhold script.[14] This is the tenant's extract or copy from the rolls of the court baron of the manor of Wallockshale, held 3 October 1693. It tells us, in Latin, that 'to this court came Thomas Darby, one of the customary tenants of this manor'. He wished to transfer to Joseph Careless of Birmingham, a whitesmith, 'all that close or parcel of arable land called by the name of the Blademill Leasowe, containing by estimation three acres, be it more or less, lying and being in Oldbury aforesaid, below the manor house and between the land of Joseph Careless and the lane called Watery Lane, leading from Oldbury Green towards Bromford Bridge and now in the possession of Joseph Careless'. It will be noticed that the Careless family continued to hold the land around the Bromford Mill for the next hundred years and were the owners of the mill itself for over 70 years.

The map of 1767 which shows the proposed line of the Brindley Canal shows Blakeley Hall and the Bromford Mill, shown as Taylor's Mill, but not the Blakeley Mill, which was most probably still existing at that time. The construction of the canal obliterated the stream from the Spon Lane side and at the same time, by means of a conduit in part underground, the headwaters of the Titford-Langley stream were diverted to feed the canal in the summit area near to Roebuck Lane. Thus these upper mills were deprived of much, if not all, of their power.

The various editions of Wm. Yates's map, 1775-94, do not show any of these mills, though they do show certain details of the area, including the diversion of the Titford stream. It is probably due to the fact that this area round Oldbury was outside the County of Stafford, the mapping of which was the primary purpose of the map, and consequently was surveyed in less detail.

A sketch map of 1781, names the Bromford Mill as Oldbury Forge, and the Oldbury or Blakeley Mill as Shenston's Corn Mill.[15] It also marks, further up stream Hill's Corn Mill. Since the Spon Lane feeder had disappeared, this mill must have been on the Oldbury Green site or at the Langley site. Such is the sketch that it is not possible to decide which.

Another sketch map made by Roger Holmes in 1785, shows the two streams entering the Bromford Mill dam, the one from Oldbury Green and the other from Shenston's Mill, that is, Blakeley.[16]

The Dawson 2in. map of 1816 indicates the Titford canal reservoir, the Langley mill pool, and what may have been the remains of a pool in the Oldbury Green area. There is no sign of the Blakeley site and the only relevant name is Millfold at Langley.

The first edition 1in. O.S. map of 1831 shows that the Green area had been built over and there was no trace of the Blakeley Mill. The Langley Mill and pool were marked and named.

The Oldbury and Langley Tithe map of 1845 marks and names the Langley Mill Pool and the Bromford Pool, and though there is a slight indication of what might have been the remains of a pool a little above Oldbury Green, the site was no longer used.

A map of Oldbury and Langley of 1857, by John W. Bates is contained in *Picturesque Oldbury* by Henry McKean, published in 1900. This clearly marks and names Langley Mill and pool, so presumably it was still operating at that date. If so, it was the only one. The only indication of the Blakeley Mill is the existence of Mill Farm marked five chains east of the Anchor canal bridge.

A small estate map drawn in 1876 by J. Cooksey, shows that the Langley Mill had gone though the dam continued to exist.

The remains of the Mill Farm at Blakeley could still be seen until the construction of the M5 link motorway in 1969. At the Langley site, though the pool was filled in to provide a private car park for the firm of Albright and Wilson, there still stood a building on the site of the mill and known as mill house until 1966.

NOTES

1.   F. W. Hackwood, *Oldbury and Roundabout* (1915), p. 47.
2.   Halesowen Manorial Court Roll, 1293; *Trans. Worcs. Hist. Soc.*, vol. 1, p. 225.
3.   *Ibid.*, 1294; *Ibid.*, p. 280.
4.   *Ibid.*, 1297; *Ibid.*, p. 336.
5.   *Ibid.*, 1300; *Ibid.*, p. 548.
6.   *Ibid.*, 1302; *Trans. Worcs. Hist. Soc.*, vol. 3, p. 128.
7.   *Ibid.*, 1302; *Trans. Worcs. Hist. Soc.*, vol. 1, p. 449.
8.   *Ibid.*, 1302; *Ibid.*, p. 443.
9.   F. W. Hackwood, *Oldbury and Roundabout* (1915), p. 81.
10.   West Bromwich Manorial Court Roll, 1573.
11.   W. F. Carter, ed., *The Midland Antiquary* (N.D.), vol. 3. p. 72.
12.   Warley Library: MS. document 1.
13.   Warley Library; MS. document 7.
14.   Birmingham Reference Library, 324254.
15.   Stafford County Record Office, Q/SB A.1781.
16.   Boulton Correspondence; Birmingham Assay Office.

PART FOUR

THE INDUSTRIAL CONTRIBUTION

In considering the part played by the water mills on the Upper Tame, in the growth of industry that was to be the foundation of the modern industrial conurbation, it is essential not to under-estimate the paucity of evidence which remains today. It is highly unlikely that the 48 sites, of which some account is given in this work, represent anything like the total that formerly existed. Many small undertakings, principally concerned with the grinding of corn, the sharpening of edge tools or even, at a later date, small forges, must have been established, passed a short and uneventful life and faded away leaving no trace. It must also be borne in mind that such evidence as remains, and which has been quoted in earlier chapters, is woefully thin, leaving far too many gaps in the story. Particularly is it to be regretted that exact dates for the establishment or cessation of an activity at a mill are rarely available, and we are left with estimates which may well be far from accurate in many cases.

The four mills recorded in Domesday had increased to 11 known corn mills in the course of the next two centuries. The proliferation was strictly controlled in order to preserve manorial rights, and it is probable that one at least, Walsall, was a Domesday omission. Others were due to grants made to the Church. Reference to other forms of water mill might have been expected, in particular, fulling-mills and blade-mills. However the earliest mention of a fulling-mill was that at Holford, below Perry Barr and only marginal to the area we have studied. Here, in 1368, John Botetourt granted to Roger de Wyreley permission to construct sluices for a fulling-mill.[1] There was another such in Wednesbury by 1423 and one in Walsall about the end of the 16th or beginning of the 17th century. None of these appear to have lasted long or left much of a record. Even less trace was left by blade-mills for we do not hear of these prior to the end of the 16th century. As late as the early 17th century we find 'private enterprise' in the matter of establishing new mills, being strongly discouraged.[2]

The earliest connection with the iron trade was the water-powered bloom-smithy. As described in an earlier chapter, the early bloom-smithies were man- or horse-powered and usually only temporary in siting. The date of the establishment of the various water-driven smithies is very uncertain. It is possible that the Walsall bloom-smithy and the one at Bloomfield (Tipton) date from the early 14th century and as such might well be cited as the earliest industrial establishments on permanent sites. The only two other such mills in the region were the one in Perry Barr-Holford area, operating in 1543[3] and that at Friar Park, which was probably converted from a corn mill after the dissolution of Hales Abbey in 1539. It is difficult to state at what date these smithies ceased to operate though it is certain that they became obsolete with the introduction of the open, charcoal-burning, cold-blast furnace and the finery and chafery. The Friar Park smithy was derelict in 1592 and the Walsall one ceased about 25 years later. A furnace had been established at Perry Barr before 1597. The Tipton smithy is something of a problem, for the name was still in use at the end of the 17th century and the name 'Bloom Smithy Mill' was continued until at least 1774.

The last quarter of the 16th century and the first of the 17th saw the great development of the use of water power. The Perry Barr furnace, the blast produced by water-driven bellows, was in operation in 1597. The West Bromwich furnace was built soon after 1600 and it is probable that the Rushall furnace started at about the same time. It will be noted that these were situated, in contrast to the 18th and 19th century blast-furnaces, on the eastern side of the area, where presumably charcoal was more easily available. Dud Dudley was complaining of the depletion of timber supplies around the Dudley area in the first decade of the 17th century. In his work of 1665 he was urging the use of coal in preference to wood-charcoal, but it could scarcely have been this replacement which caused the end of these three furnaces. The West Bromwich furnace had closed before 1649. Nothing is heard of the Perry Barr furnace from the end of the 16th century. On the other hand Rushall furnace persisted until at least 1788, though it had probably been rebuilt and abandoned the use of charcoal before this date. It therefore seems probable that the demise of the other two furnaces was due to inability to face competition from other large concerns, such as Aston, operating by 1615, and the Hales and Trescott Grange furnaces. These all continued to produce pig iron well into the coke era.

With the establishment of the furnace came the 'finery' and 'chafery' with their trip-hammers for the purifying of the pig iron and the working up into the raw material suitable for further processing. These were usually together under one roof and collectively termed a forge. Most of the local forges dated from the early 17th century: Holford Forge, West Bromwich Old Forge, Wednesbury Forge, Wednesbury Bridge Forge and Rushall Forge all apparently being constructed within about 20 years from 1592. It is interesting to note the later dates of erection of the forges further up stream. Bromford, originally a blade-mill, was converted to a forge at an uncertain date, probably late 17th century. Sparrow's Forge and Tipton Forge both date from the latter half of the 18th the former being converted from 'horse' to 'water' power in 1767. Bagnall's Forge commenced early in the 19th century, Friar Park about 1805, while Dunkirk Mill became a 'trip-hammer' forge in 1823. There was no one period which marked the cessation of the mills as forges, since conversion to steam power enabled some sites to continue in use long after the general decline in water power. Wednesbury Forge continues as such to this day, water power supplementing steam until early in the present century. On the other hand, the advent of steam power proved in most cases to be the end of the water-powered forge; a foundry was started at West Bromwich Hall Forge about 1790; Tipton Forge was converted to a foundry between 1812 and 1820; Wednesbury Bridge Forge was sold in 1816 and became a corn mill; West Bromwich Old Forge was sold in 1823 and ceased to operate, while Friar Park Forge, after a short life of some 25 years, was abandoned and became derelict about 1830.

The most mechanically advanced of the water mills contributing to the iron industry was the slitting-mill, which provided the rods for the nailing industry, the principal work of the Black Country in its early days. W. K. V. Gale states that such a mill was established at Dartford, in Kent, in 1588, and reminds us of the stories of 'Fiddler' Richard Foley.[4] At least the enterprise of Foley in bringing the idea to the Midlands is not in dispute. 'He erected a slitting mill at Hyde, near Stourbridge, in about 1628'. When his son, Thomas Foley, took the lease of Bustleholme Mill in 1650, it was already a slitting-mill, a purpose to which it seems to have been converted between 1628 and 1630 by the previous tenants. For long it was the only slitting- or rod-mill in the area under survey. It ceased such work about 1804, never being equipped for steam power. Towards the end of its career it had the competition—or assistance, since it was initially operated by the same manager—of a lesser known slitting-mill, Sandwell. This was converted from a corn mill to rod-slitting just prior to 1775, working under the same management as Friar Park Forge and Bustleholme Rod Mill to 1804. It was then worked in conjunction with the West Bromwich Old Forge which ceased to function in 1823.

There was no one period which may be regarded as that of the blade-mill. Such a mill required little in the way of machinery or of actual water power. While they were suitable for the smallest of brooks they were not confined to such. Bromford was a blade-mill when purchased in 1610 and remained such for something like two centuries. Bustleholme was a blade-mill at the beginning of the 17th century and reverted to that status for a few years at the beginning of the 19th. Sparrow's Forge was used by Elwell and Edwards, edge tool makers from 1812 to 1817, while Wednesbury Forge was used for saw-making about 1725 and as an edge tool works from 1817 to the present time.

Again, the rolling of iron sheet or plate does not appear to have reached any great importance so far as the water mills were concerned. From 1704 to about 1722, Wednesbury Forge was used for plating. Bustleholme was a rolling-mill from 1819 to 1830.

We can find little reference to the water mills being used for what might be regarded as the end products of an industry, apart from edge tools. The making of saws at Wednesbury Forge around 1725 has already been referred to and we find the same factory being used for the grinding of gun-barrels, some 70 years later. Another example would be the wire mills which were to be found at Bromford about 1780 and at Grete about 1835.

While a few mills, like Joan Mill, Hamstead, Walsall Town and Walsall New Mill remained water corn mills throughout their existence, few of those which had taken part in any other activity, reverted to that function. West Bromwich Old Forge, Bustleholme, Rushall and Wednesbury Bridge Mills were the exceptions. These were all re-converted to corn mills in the period from 1800 to 1829. Despite the ever-increasing competition from steam flour mills, these struggled on until towards the close of the century, Bustleholme and Old Forge Mills still working as grist-mills grinding cattle food for local farmers until the First World War.

For the rest, they were lost for ever in the spread of 19th-century industrial sprawl.

Thus we have seen the work to which these mills were put throughout their lives. We have seen them bloom and fade, but to what extent did they affect the area and the lives of the people who dwelt there?

In regarding this aspect we may dismiss from our consideration those which were grinding corn, sawing timber or engaged in fulling cloth, for these, like hundreds of others throughout the land, were providing the necessities of life for urban and rural community alike and only influenced a limited locality. It was the mill occupied with the iron trade which was the speciality of the Midland plateau, though not its peculiarity, for Sussex, the Forest of Dean and other areas shared the industry.

We have noted that the work in iron was well established by the 14th century. The assignment of dower of Juliana Heronville of Wednesbury in 1315 includes coal-pits and iron mines in the property.[5] When Thomas Reignald of Tipton sued William and Agnes Yolbragge in 1395 for the spoliation of his estates during his nonage, he claimed that they had removed '1,000 cartlads of ironstone and 1,000 cartlads of seacole'.[6] A number of smiths are to be found in the records and by mid-century Spourier, Sporyour (Spurrier?) had become a family name in Walsall.[7] Already the degree of specialisation within the area, referred to by Dr. Plot, was to be found.[8] The better ores of Rushall and Walsall were used by the loriners of Walsall and the locksmiths of Willenhall while the poorer ores of Wednesbury produced the 'blend metal' suitable only for nail-making. Throughout the 14th and 15th centuries the iron rod was produced almost entirely by the itinerant bloom-smiths so far as we can see, though a few fixed sites appear to have been used, as indicated above.

The people who produced the finished articles, the nails, locks, buckles and spurs, were at first the husbandman who sought to augment a meagre existence by part-time work in his own home. Later, as population increased, particularly after the lean decade which followed the

Black Death, this industry attracted many, those who were landless, those who preferred to avoid the hardship of inclement weather and particularly those who wished to be self-employed even though the income and living standard were likely to be little improved. It was an industry which called for little capital outlay. At the end of the 18th century James Keir described the nailmaking as requiring 'a very simple apparatus of a small hearth, bellows, anvil and hammer. It is executed at the workman's own house, to each of which houses a small nailing shop is annexed, where the man, his wife and children can work without going home; and thus an existence is given to an uncommon multitude of small houses and cottages scattered all over the country, and to a great degree of population, independently of towns'.[9]

It is not possible today to estimate accurately the numbers engaged in this work at that period, nor the quantity of iron consumed. Dud Dudley, in 1665, claimed 'within ten miles of Dudley there be nearly 20,000 smiths of all sorts'.[10] In 1799 it was estimated that there were 35-40,000 nailers in the region, consuming 10,000 tons of iron per annum.[11] Even if we allow only one third of these estimates as living in the Tame valley and the rest in the Stour valley, these figures might seem surprisingly high when we consider that the total population of the Tame area of the Black Country as late as 1801 was little over 31,000. Yet there can be no doubt of the high percentage of the population so involved. An examination of the parish registers provides a clue. In the period 1653-9 inclusive, there are mentioned in the West Bromwich parish registers, 195 nailers, 42 other ironworkers compared with a total of 133 for all other occupations. Coal-mining did not develop here until the beginning of the 19th century. In Wednesbury for the years 1678-99 we have 73 colliers, 83 nailers, 20 other ironworkers as against 75 other trades. The decade 1720-9 inclusive provides us with the interesting distribution in Bilston of nine colliers, nine nailers, 186 buckle-makers and 48 chape (buckle tongue) makers, about 100 other ironworkers including 28 locksmiths and 20 gunlock-filers, both mainly from Willenhall, and 17 iron-box makers, as a contrast to 177 other occupations. The predominance of the small part iron-working artisan is indisputable. These men were for much of the time dependant on the 'ironmonger' or middleman who provided the iron rod and purchased the finished produce from the workmen. Undoubtedly it was largely the malpractices on the part of these middlemen that caused the hardship and at times unrest among these craftsmen. Despite the poor returns, there was no shortage of newcomers into the trades. Attempts were made to restrict the increase in numbers. The Statute of Apprentices and Artificers in 1563 provided for a compulsory seven-year service as an apprentice to be undertaken only by a member of the master's household. Throughout the rest of the century there were numerous cases in which small-holding farmers were fined for practising these crafts, half of the fine going to the informant.[12] The West Bromwich Manorial Court of 1606 ordered that 'no inhabitant within this manor using the trade, mystery or occupation of a smith, naylor or bucklemaker shall set or let any stall or stock to any person or persons of the same trade or occupation to work upon contrary to the Statute upon risk of a fine of 6s. 8d. In order to reduce the risk of dependence on the parish it was also ordered that no resident should give shelter to anyone from another parish without first giving to the churchwardens a guarantee of indemnity. These precautions were unavailing. As late as October 1687 there were 71 cases of encroachment of the Lord's Wastes (the commons) 26 of which were concerned with the building of work-shops.[13]

We have stated above that these workmen were supplied by the ironmongers. These in turn obtained their stock from the forges and slitting-mills which dealt with the pig iron from the furnaces. Already it has been shown that the furnaces within our immediate area were the early open type, greedy in the use of charcoal, small and inefficient. The five main suppliers in 1717 were the blast furnaces at Hales (Halesowen), Grange, Aston, Cradley and Pool Bank and their output was only some 1,850 tons per annum of which Hales produced about 500 tons.[14] It is obvious that that amount was insufficient and that considerable quantities were brought in from outside. The Foley Partnership were bringing more than 1,000 tons a year of pig iron from their furnaces in the Forest of Dean.

If the furnaces were insufficient, what of the forges? The output of the Tame forges was small indeed. For the six years 1667-72 the average output from the Wednesbury Forge was about 111 tons while that from the West Bromwich Forge was 176 tons.[15] Such quantities could not meet the demand and the ironmongers had to turn to forges outside the region. For the most part these were the Stour valley forges, despite the cost of carriage. In 1688-9 carriage from the Stour forges to Wednesbury was 21s. per ton, to West Bromwich 22s. 6d. and to Tipton from 22s. 6d. to 24s.[16] Two of the largest purchasers were the Wednesbury merchants Henry Fidoe, 49 tons, and Bayley Brett, 30 tons. A later Bayley Brett acquired his own forge, the Hall Mill Forge at West Bromwich (*q.v.*) in 1751. Even the Stour forges could not always meet the demand for though John Jennens appears as a chapman on the sales accounts of the Stour forges from 1691 to 1701, yet he had to look much further afield. In 1692-3 he purchased 10 tons of bar from the Chartley Forge in North Staffordshire for despatch to Bustleholme for slitting.[17] Similarly, in the Rugeley slitting-mill accounts for the year 1694-5 we find,[18]

	Moorland Rod		Coldshort Rod	
	tons	cwt.	tons	cwt.
Bayley Brett, West Bromwich	53	19	28	16
John Lowe, ,, ,,		10	8	10
Benjamin Lowe, ,,		10		10

All of the above were purchasing bar and rod from the Stour complex. Coldshort rod was nail material.

If the Tame forges were unable to supply the local needs, the slitting-mill was in no better position. From 1667 to 1672 Bustleholme took the whole of the bar iron from Wednesbury Forge but little more. As mentioned above, during the Jennens period at the end of the century Bustleholme was slitting small quantities from other sources. After its acquisition by the Lowe family in 1709, a forge was set up to work with the rod-mill, and pig iron was purchased both from the Hales furnace and from the Aston furnace after its acquisition by the Knights in 1747. Nevertheless, the quantities were small, for example:

				Hales		Aston	
				tons	cwt.	tons	cwt.
1727 ..	..	..	..	2	8	—	—
1751 ..	..	..	..	2	6	—	—
1752 ..	..	..	..	—	—	1	2½[19]

After Wright and Jesson had taken over West Bromwich Old Forge *c.* 1765 it was converted to West Bromwich Rolling and Slitting Mill. Matthew Boulton visited the site in 1785 with a view to giving advice on ways of improving its output.[20] He noted that it was operated by a foreman and three workmen who could heat, roll, slit and bundle three tons of rod in a 12-hour day. Accordingly he estimated that the annual output working a six-day week, for 50 weeks a year, was 900 tons. He stated that it was impossible to increase the furnace capacity due to the lack of water power available but that the output might be quadrupled by the introduction of a steam mill. His conclusion was 'Bromwich Mill is a trifling Mill'.

Such, I am afraid, must be our conclusion in respect of the ironworks of the 14th to 19th centuries, where water supplied the power. It was only at Horseley and Wednesbury Forge, where steam first supplemented and only later supplanted water power, that work continued in a relatively uninterrupted manner.

The water mills of this area made their contribution, an important one at the time, to the growing iron industry but at no time did they completely fill its needs.

NOTES

1.   *V.C.H., Warws.*, vol. 7 (1964), p. 255.
2.   West Bromwich Manorial Court Roll, 15 Jas. I.
3.   *V.C.H., Warws.*, vol. 7 (1964), p. 257.
4.   W. K. V. Gale, *B.R.S.*, p. 196.
5.   *S.H.C.* (1911), pp. 321-23.
6.   *S.H.C.*, vol. XV, p. 68.
7.   Walsall Calendar of Deeds, Nos. 45 and 53.
8.   Plot, *op. cit.*, ch. 4, para 20.
9.   *See* Tipton Bloomsmithy Mill; Stebbing Shaw, *op. cit.*, James Keir's contribution.
10.   Dud Dudley, *Martellum Martis* (1665), p. 62.
11.   T. Nash, *Collections for a History of Worcestershire* (1799); M. J. Wise and B. L. C. Johnson, *B.R.S.*, p. 172.
12.   *Staffordshire Quarter Sessions Rolls*, 1589 (*S.H.C.*, 1930, p. 102); 1594 (*S.H.C.*, 1932, p. 60); 1597 (*S.H.C.*, 1935, p. 45).
13.   West Bromwich Manorial Court Roll, October 1687.
14.   M. J. Wise and B. L. C. Johnson, *B.R.S.*, p. 169.
15.   Hereford County Record Office; F/VI/MAF/35.
16.   *Ibid.*, F/VI/GAF/35. Rod Iron Account, 1688-9.
17.   B. L. C. Johnson, *Charcoal Iron Trade of the Midlands, 1690-1720* (n.d.), p. 128.
18.   *Ibid.*, appendix 19.
19.   Knight's Account Books.
20.   Matthew Boulton's Note Book, 1785; Birmingham Assay Office.

APPENDIX ONE

Extract from Mill Schedule, Bustleholme Mill, 1819

Oak timber Pounstables and Forebay with aperture.

Paddle, Starts and Geering.

Oak timber Pounstables and Stop Gate at the back of the Mill.

Cast iron waterwheel with three rings.

Wrought iron floats or ladles, fastened with wrought Iron Pins.

Cast iron Shaft with turned nocks on Cast iron Headstocks and Brass Brasses fixed with wrought iron holddown pins on substantial timber Carriages.

Cast iron main driving wheel on Water Wheel axis and Pinion Wheel to suit on Fly Wheel Shaft.

Cast iron Fly Wheel 'Socket and Arms' on ditto Shaft with turned nocks on Cast iron Head Stocks and Brass Brasses affixed as above with Wrought iron hold down Pins.

Note, The above machinery is new and complete in every respect.

Bricks under Roll bed framing

APPENDIX TWO

Extract from Mill Schedule, Bustleholme Mill, 1839

3 pairs of french stones with casings.

2 stone wedges and blocks.

Gearing to 3 mills complete.

1 Trow to Bean Mill.

1 Bean Mill.

1 fine flour cylinder in work.

1 do. not in work.

2 Smutter Bonds.

1 Machine Bond.

1 dressing Mill Bond.

1 lifting jack Bond.

3 Stretchers.

8 pr. slide ropes.

12 sieves.

1 Ten step ladder in Smutter roof.

APPENDIX THREE
Extract from Mill Schedule, Bustleholme Mill, 1860

New Water wheel with curved ladles, 17 ft. diameter and 7 ft. wide. Ladles of wrought iron ¼in. thick, and wrought iron starts. Cast iron rings, arms, sockets; hollow cylindrical shaft with base plates, plummer blocks and brasses complete.
A cast iron Sluice Gate.

APPENDIX FOUR

A list of customers of Thomas Jesson, West Bromwich, ironmonger and nail merchant, 1712-1750

Mr. Jno. Jackson, Iron Monger in Ye Poultry, London.

Mr. Jno. Woolaston, neare ye Swan Tavern in White Cross Street, London.

Mr. Antho. Ireland, Against ye White Horse at Mile End, Neare London.

Mr. Richd. Smithson, Against Bull Staires on ye Bank Side, Southwarke, London.

Mr. Willm. Hall, In King Street, Westminster, London.

Mr. Jos. Gynes, Ironmonger in Distaff Lane, London.

Mr. Mathw. Johnson, Ironmonger in Leaden Hall Street, London.

Mr. Tho. Maynard, Ironmonger in Queen Hill, London.

Mr. Edmd. Round, Thames Street, London.

Mr. Ja. Richards, on St Margaret's Hill, Southwarke, London.

Mr. Jos. Partridge, Ironmonger in St. Gylses, London.

Mr. Robt. Sparke, in Ye Strand, London.

Mr. Zach. Gisbourne, Ironmonger in Cattleton Street, London.

Mr. Josh. Wallford, without Newgate, London.

Mr. Saml. Dicke, at ye Castle in Broad Street, London.

Mr. Robt. Withall, in Guildford, Surry via London.

GLOSSARY

Armiger. An esquire; originally one who carried a knight's shield; in later usage, one entitled to bear heraldic arms.

Bereuuic (bereuuicus, -a, berewick). A demesne farm; a hamlet or member of a manor; essentially a corn-farm.

Blade-mill. A mill erected for the grinding or sharpening of blades, swords, cutlery or other edge tools.

Bloom. An ingot, ball or lump of iron having undergone the first hammering.

Bloomer. A smith whose work was the making of blooms.

Bloom-smithy. A forge or smithy where blooms were made.

Bloomery. The first forge in an ironworks through which the iron would pass from the furnace.

Breast-wheel. A waterwheel in which the water is admitted to the wheel at more or less the level of the axle.

Burr-stone. A siliceous rock used for the making of mill stones, frequently imported from France.

Chafery. One of the forges in an ironworks, on which the iron bloom was reheated in order to soften it for hammering into shape.

Demesne. The lands attached to the manor house; the home farm.

Finery. A forge or hearth on which the iron pigs were reduced to a semi-molten condition before hammering to remove impurities and produce blooms.

Fleam. Variant of flume; artificial channel, watercourse, mill-stream.

Forge. An open hearth with bellows attached, used for heating metal to render it malleable.

Fulling-mill. A mill in which cloth was fulled or milled by being beaten with wooden mallets in order to clean and thicken it or felt or mat the fibres.

Head-race. The race or flume which brings the water to the mill-wheel.

Herriot (heriot, har(r)iot). A feudal service; a render of the best beast or dead chattel of a deceased tenant due by legal custom to the lord of whom he held his tenement.

Inquisition post mortem. An investigation or inquiry as to the possessions of the deceased.

Ironmonger. A dealer in iron or iron rod.

Lade. A channel constructed to lead water from the river to the water-mill.

Leat. A water conduit; *see* 'lade'.

Mill-suit. The obligatory attendance by tenants at a certain mill, usually the manorial mill, for the purpose of grinding their corn.

Moiety. One half share.

Nick-point. A constriction in the course of a stream, a point at which the velocity of the water increases.

Overshot-wheel. A waterwheel driven by water from above.

Pannage. A right or privilege of feeding swine in the forest.

Pound. (a) An enclosure for the detention of straying or trespassing cattle; (b) a body of water confined by a dam as in a mill pond or the stretch of water in a canal above a lock; the impounded water.

Seised of. Possessed of.

Sow and Pigs. The mass of rough iron formed by the cooling of the molten iron from the furnace in a trench or groove on a sand floor. The large central groove formed the sow and the smaller subsidiary grooves the pigs.

Stank. A pond or pool; the mill-dam, or mill-pool

Tail-race. The part of the mill race below the wheel; the channel carrying the water away from the mill-wheel.

Tallage. An arbitary tax levied on feudal dependants by their superiors.

Trip-hammer. The primitive mechanism of a forge whereby the heavy hammer was raised by a cam operated by a waterwheel.

Undershot-wheel. A waterwheel driven by the water passing under it.

Walk-mill. (a) A fulling-mill (*q.v.*), from the fact that originally the cloth was walked or trodden on in a trough of water with fuller's earth; (b) a mechanical contrivance or machine the driving power of which was furnished by the walking of a horse, i.e., a horse mill.

Whitesmith. A smith who worked in metals other than iron, usually tin, as distinct from a blacksmith who worked in iron; a tinsmith.

BIBLIOGRAPHY

G. C. Allen, *The Industrial Development of Birmingham and the Black Country*, 1860-1927 (1966).

M. J. Wise, ed., *Birmingham and its Regional Setting* (1950).

W. H. B. Court, *The Rise of Midland Industries, 1600-1838* (1938).

J. F. Ede, *The History of Wednesbury* (1962).

Chas. J. L. Elwell, *The Iron Elwells* (1964).

S. Griffiths, *Guide to the Iron Trade of Great Britain* (1873).

F. W. Hackwood, *History of Handsworth* (1908).

F. W. Hackwood, *Oldbury and Round About* (1915).

F. W. Hackwood, *History of Tipton* (1891).

F. W. Hackwood, *Wednesbury, Ancient and Modern* (1902).

F. W. Hackwood, *History of West Bromwich* (1895).

F. W. Hackwood, *Wednesbury Workshops* (1889).

E. J. Homeshaw, *The Boroughs and Foreign of Walsall* (1960).

G. R. Morton and M. le Guillou, 'The rise and fall of the South Staffordshire pig iron industry' in The British Foundryman (July 1967), p. 269.

G. R. Morton and J. Gould, 'Little Aston Forge; 1574-1798,' in *Journal of the Iron and Steel Institute*, vol. 205 (March 1967), p. 237.

John Parkes, *History of Tipton* (1915).

Dr. Robert Plot, *Natural History of Staffordshire* (1686).

Joseph Reeves, *History of West Bromwich* (1836).

Rev. Stebbing Shaw, *Natural History of Staffordshire* (1798).

S. Timmins, *Birmingham and Midland Hardware Industries* (1866).

M. Willett, *History of West Bromwich* (1882).

F. W. Willmore, *History of Walsall* (1881).

INDEX